DEBRETT'S

REVIEW OF THE YEAR

200

Debrett's Review 2007
Published by Debrett's Limited
18–20 Hill Rise, Richmond,
Surrey TW10 6UA
United Kingdom

Managing Editor Jo Bryant

Editorial Assistants Sarah Corney, Ellie Major

Head of Publishing Elizabeth Wyse

Page design Karen Wilks
Page layout Design 23
Cover design LASH&KO

Proof reading and additional research Ruth Massey

ISBN 978 1 870520 812

Printed and bound in Great Britain by Butler and Tanner, Frome.

Visit us as www.debretts.co.uk

DEBRETT'S

REVIEW OF THE YEAR 2007

INTRODUCTION

THE YEAR OF...

PEOPLE IN THE NEWS

REVIEW OF THE YEAR

2007

INTRODUCTION

The year has been packed with a dazzling array of achievements, stories, disasters, embarrassments, scandals, joy and tragedy. In this book we have set out to distill the essence of the year, providing an unforgettable snapshot of Britain, and the British, in 2007. We hope that the book will be revisited in the years to come – a nostalgic, and unexpected, evocation of a unique 12 months.

2007 has been captured in over 200 pages of text, and over 300 colour photographs. We have invited some uniquely well-qualified commentators, including Gabby Logan and Sir Andrew Lloyd Webber, to share their memories of the year with us. Words, pictures, facts and quotes all contribute to this unique record. Sometimes the pictures just speak for themselves.

It has been an immense challenge to capture such an action-packed year in words and pictures, and inevitably some stories have not made it to these pages. We are not aiming to provide a comprehensive guide to the 365 days of 2007, rather we are offering our own insight. We would love to hear what you, our readers, think – email us at publications@debretts.co.uk.

Stories are grouped under headings – People in the News, Music and Fashion, Sport, and so on – but are not arranged chronologically. We hope you will see this book as a lucky dip, an invitation to browse, with surprises and revelations on every page.

Putting this book together has been exciting and daunting. We think the effort has been worthwhile, and hope that you will enjoy reading it as much as we have enjoyed compiling it.

2008 is another year, another set of stories, and another Debrett's Review just waiting to happen!

THE YEAR

"this man changed history"

"the top twenty is a reflection of our changing needs"

OF...

"becoming carbon neutral is only the beginning"

"a momentous decision: MySpace or Facebook?"

MAPPINS ROAD

TELEPHONE

WACKY
WEATHER

2007 IS ON ITS WAY TO BEING THE SECOND-WARMEST YEAR SINCE RECORDS BEGAN IN THE 1860S.

Winter 2006–07 and spring 2007 were the mildest on record, but in June and July torrential rains lashed the country, causing an estimated £2.7 billion of damage.

Summer 2007 was the wettest since records began in 1914.

Record-breaking weather suggests that Britain's weather patterns are changing in a manner consistent with predictions of climate change, which forecast rising temperatures and rainfall as global warming increases.

THE (WET) SEASON

The traditional British Social Season was a washout, with rain, mud and grey skies dominating the annual glamorous sporting fixtures such as Ascot and Henley.

19–23 JUNE: ROYAL ASCOT
High winds and rain played havoc with ladies' hats.

4–8 JULY: HENLEY ROYAL REGATTA
The strict dress code was relaxed, and visitors were allowed to wear wellington boots for the first time.

GINS Link O'Rama Mail Windows

facebook

Profile

Search ▾

Q

Applications

News

Groups

Photos

Events

Marketplace

FACEBOOK

The social networking site became the hottest thing to do on the net in 2007. It's part diary, part photo album, part messaging service, and part gossip machine.

Surfing around on a networking site has become the digital equivalent of loitering outside the chippy for today's teens, who load their profile with photos, news about music groups and detailed explanations of their likes and dislikes. There are an estimated 300 sites making up the cyber networking universe.

Originally called thefacebook, Facebook was founded in 2004 by former Harvard student Mark Zuckerberg who ran it as a hobby. It began life as a social networking tool at Harvard University, and rapidly grew to prominence. Rumours of an acquisition continue to circulate, with some estimates putting the value of the social network at £5 billion.

Facebook is the UK's most popular social network on the web, and lags behind only MySpace in terms of global traffic.

"There comes a time in every young person's life – soon after teething, usually – when she must make a momentous decision: MySpace or Facebook?" Christopher Beam, online magazine *Slate*

FACE THE FACTS

The name refers to the paper facebooks of the campus community that US colleges and preparatory schools give to incoming students, faculty and staff

In August 2005, thefacebook was officially named Facebook and the domain facebook.com was purchased for a reported $200,000

At the time of going to press there are approximately 42 million active users worldwide, and four million in the UK

There have been more than 100,000 new registrations per day since January 2007

Active users have doubled since Facebook expanded registration in September 2006

The site receives over 15 billion page views per month

It currently hosts over 1.7 billion photos

More than 70 per cent of UK employers are now blocking their employees from using social network sites at work, an activity known as 'faceblocking'

SUPER
BRANDS

13 September: Aston Martin came top in a survey of
the coolest brands in the UK compiled by CoolBrands,
a programme run by the Superbrands organisation.
The results showed an interesting mix of old and new.

"The top twenty is a reflection of our changing needs, wants and
interests… on the one hand, things can become cool by virtue of their
necessity or prevalence in your life, like Google, or Amazon. On the
other, the things you really want, but may know you'll never get
– like a Rolex or a Ferrari – are considered just as cool."
Stephen Cheliotis, chairman, CoolBrands Council

STREET ART

The National Gallery used MP3 downloads to guide the public around an innovative outdoor art exhibition.

12 June–31 August: The National Gallery's Grand Tour – a play on the 17th-century cultural tours of Europe – aimed to bring art to the people, free of the constraints of galleries.

Over 30 reproductions of major works of art were exhibited in unexpected places, transfixing passers-by in the streets of Soho, Piccadilly and Covent Garden.

Various audioguides were offered, either by an MP3 download from the Gallery's website, or by phoning a number displayed by each painting for pre-recorded information on the work. Works included Van Gogh's Sunflowers, Constable's The Hay Wain, Stubbs's Whistlejacket, Monet's The Water-Lily Pond, and Botticelli's Venus and Mars.

NO
SMOKING
JULY 1 2007

SMOKEFREE
BRITAIN

1 July: NO SMOKING

England joined the rest of the UK in banning smoking in public spaces. Scotland forged ahead on 26 March 2006, Wales on 2 April 2007, and Northern Ireland on 30 April 2007.

MARCH ON BRITAIN

THE FIRST EMPEROR:
CHINA'S TERRACOTTA ARMY
British Museum
13 September 2007 – 6 April 2008

"This man changed history.
This man made China,
created the idea of China."

Neil MacGregor,

British Museum Director

There was a huge sense of anticipation over the exhibition of terracotta warriors buried in the tomb of China's first emperor, Qin Shihuangdi, which opened at the British Museum on 13 September.

With a total of 150,403 tickets sold in advance, the show looks set to beat the record-breaking Tutankhamun exhibition of 1972, seen by 1.7 million people.

Approximately 8,000 terracotta figures were discovered by two farmers in a remote part of Shaanxi province in 1974.

The life-sized figures form an exact reproduction of the first emperor's victorious forces, and were placed in his tomb in readiness for the afterlife.

The exhibition, an outstanding example of ongoing cultural collaboration between China and the UK, is the culmination of years of careful diplomacy by curator Jane Portal, who has negotiated the loan of about 20 figures and associated objects.

BLOOD MOON

3 March: The total lunar eclipse was visible from large portions of the UK, thanks to clear skies. The moon took on a coppery-red hue and stunned star-gazers around the world.

"One of the best lunar eclipses from Britain for years."
Robin Scagell, Society for Popular Astronomy

"Becoming carbon neutral is only the beginning. The climate problem will not be solved by one company reducing its emissions to zero, and it won't be solved by one government acting alone. The climate problem will not be solved without mass participation by the general public in countries around the globe." Rupert Murdoch

THINK GREEN

2007 was the year when consumers became preoccupied with carbon offsetting, shopping bag wars, food miles and campaigns to choose fresh, locally produced food.

CARBON COMPENSATION

In September, a survey by the British Market Research Bureau revealed that two per cent of respondents were under the impression that carbon offsetting was a 'new technique that eases trapped wind caused by carbonated/fizzy drinks'.

Just over 50 per cent of 15 to 24-year-olds had never heard of it. Carbon offsetting involves individuals or companies attempting to compensate for their contribution to global warming, such as planting trees, pumping greenhouse gases underground and setting up green energy projects abroad.

CELEB 'CARBON CRIMINALS'

In January, the BBC named and shamed celebrity 'carbon criminals' in a programme entitled *Should I Really Give Up Flying?* Private jet users including Simon Cowell and Sharon Osbourne were castigated for their love of luxury flying.

It is estimated that David Beckham is emitting 15,000kg of carbon emissions a year. Tom Cruise is said to own three private jets; he's so disliked by the eco-lobby that he has been dubbed 'Emissions Impossible'.

THE ANTIPLASTIC MOVEMENT

150,000,000 plastic bags are used in the UK every week – each one takes around 100 years to rot away in a landfill site.

In 2007, the 'It' shopping bag was born. Designers including Anya Hindmarch, Stella McCartney and Louis Vuitton launched reusable shoppers.

Waitrose, Asda, Tesco, Sainsbury's and other supermarkets now all offer their customers 'bags for life' for just a few pence.

LOCAL FOOD

2007 was the year that the organic vegetable box became more widely available – Sainsbury's launched the first supermarket organic box. Consumer pressure has also helped the notion of 'eating organic'.

Supermarkets reported a huge rise in sales of organic produce over the past year, and have been forced to rethink. They are now sourcing local foods from local farmers, offering alternatives to products from far-off lands which are air-freighted – 'food miles' became a new preoccupation. Ethical shoppers are advised to buy local and choose produce farmed in this country.

CLIMATE CHANGE MATTERS

Jonathon Porritt, Founder Director of Forum for the Future and Chairman of the UK Sustainable Development Commission, argues that more general awareness of the reality of climate change is a reason to be hopeful.

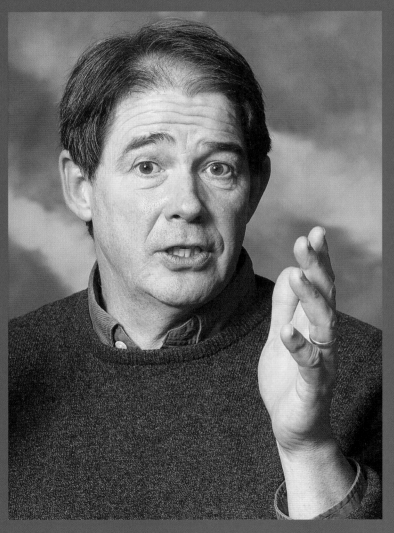

In June and July 2007, the heavens opened, and many parts of England were subject to the worst flooding in recorded history. The personal suffering was considerable; the insurance bills cataclysmic. Inevitably, debate raged between those inclined to blame the floods directly on accelerating climate change, and those who steadfastly refused to acknowledge that there was any direct cause-and-effect at all.

Self-respecting scientists are loath to put their hands on their hearts and declare that any one particular flood, drought, hurricane, firestorm or heatwave is a direct consequence of the build up of CO_2 and other greenhouse gases in the atmosphere over the last two decades. There are now, however, very few scientists who believe there is no connection at all between the rising emissions of those gases and the countless extreme weather events that the world is currently witnessing. Apart from a few die-hard deniers, the basic 'truth' of climate change is no longer in dispute.

The title of Al Gore's Oscar-winning film, *An Inconvenient Truth*, accurately captures what many feel about this development. Over the last couple of years climate change has placed itself bang in the middle of contemporary politics, cutting right across every aspiration politicians may have, and making the business of building a safer, more prosperous world for everyone a great deal more complicated. Indeed, it seems inevitable that the complex challenges of dealing with climate change will command more and more political space as the years go by.

Even just a few years ago, the majority of people would have seen such assertions as both politically contentious and scientifically 'dodgy'. Now I would expect that most people would find themselves in broad agreement.

That our generation seems to have leapt, in one fell swoop, from denial to despair is particularly disempowering for young people. If you subscribe to that uplifting aphorism that 'we do not inherit the Earth from our parents, but borrow it from our children', then we've made a real mess of things, and now seem intent on stealing whatever reasons the people of tomorrow might still have to be hopeful.

Apart from a few die-hard deniers, the basic 'truth' of climate change is no longer in dispute.

So on what grounds can optimism still be justified? For the best part of fifteen years, I have been fortunate enough to work with a large number of people at senior level in many fields across government and business – through Forum for the Future, the UK Sustainable Development Commission and The Prince of Wales's Business and the Environment Programme. My overwhelming impression is that more and more of them are now determined to find more sustainable ways of doing their jobs.

The change of heart amongst business people is particularly encouraging. For many of them, sustainable development has been positioned in the wrong psychological box over all these years – the one labelled 'regulation and red tape', 'constraint on business', 'increased costs' or 'high risk'. Only during the last few years have we seen the other box – labelled 'opportunity', 'innovation', 'increased market share' and 'stronger brands' – opening up in such a way as to provide wealth creators with an entirely different and far more positive proposition. This is critical: however necessary or desirable something may be, it is unlikely to obtain the necessary traction in today's world unless the business community can be persuaded and inspired to get behind it.

This gathering awareness is both extremely welcome and timely – in that there is still time to make a real difference. I am not one of those who believe it's all too late; the bad news about climate change does indeed go on getting worse, but allowing our civilisation to collapse is not yet our destiny. As long as we get moving without further delay!

WORD GAMES

2007 saw the publication of two monumental works of reference: on 4 June the *Collins English Dictionary* (9th edition, with 1,500 new words) and, on 20 September, *The Shorter Oxford English Dictionary* (6th edition, with 2,500 new words). Teams of lexicographers have been monitoring the words that have entered the language, which reflect a number of modern concerns: celebrity culture, green issues, new technology, and multi-ethnicity.

ADDY: an email address

ADULTESCENT: an adult still actively interested in youth culture

BROMANCE: an intimate but non-sexual relationship between two men

CARBON FOOTPRINT: the amount of greenhouse gas emissions an individual is responsible for

CARBON NEUTRAL: achieving a zero level of carbon dioxide emissions

CATTLE CLASS: economy seats on an aircraft

CELEBUTANTES: heiresses who become celebrities

CHAV: a young working class person who dresses in sports clothing

CHELSEA TRACTOR: a petrol-guzzling 4x4

GREEN AUDIT: an inspection of a company to assess its impact on the environment

HEAVIOSITY: the quality of being serious, intense or 'heavy', especially in popular music

HOODIE: young person wearing a hooded sweatshirt

KHEER: an Indian dessert of rice and sweet milk

McMANSION: a large modern house with a mass-produced appearance

MANBAG: a man's handbag or shoulder bag

MAN FLU: the male tendency to talk up the symptoms of the common cold

MUFFIN TOP: bulging stomach protruding over low-rise jeans

PAPPING: the taking of photographs by the paparazzi

PASTILLA: a Moroccan pigeon pie

SEASON CREEP: the changing length of the seasons, thought to be caused by climate change

SIZE ZERO: a very small size in women's clothes, equating to UK size 4

TANOREXIC: a person who is obsessed with maintaining a permanent tan

VLOG: an internet video journal

WAG: the wife or girlfriend of a famous sportsman

WEBINAR: a seminar conducted on the internet

WHOVIAN: a fan of the television series *Doctor Who*

YUMMY MUMMY: an attractive mother

SILLY

Beastly

9 JUNE: Photographs of a large, hairy four-legged creature, spotted near a group of schoolchildren on Dartmoor, were actually claimed to be of a pet Newfoundland dog named Troy, belonging to a local family. The photographs were taken by falconer Martin Whitley, who claimed that the animal was a big cat; others thought it was a wild boar.

"The creature I saw was black and grey and comparable in size to a miniature pony. It had very thick shoulders, a long, thick tail with a blunt end and small round ears." Martin Whitley

Jellygate

29 JULY: Tempers flared at the second India *v* England test match, when a row erupted over jelly beans on the pitch. The sweets were tossed on the pitch when tail-end batsman Zaheer Khan was batting. The No. 9 batsman, who believed the jelly beans were being deliberately thrown at the crease, brandished his bat angrily at Kevin Pietersen. The row was just one of a number of angry exchanges between the two sides as tempers became frazzled.

"Zaheer wasn't too pleased. I think he prefers blue jelly beans to the pink ones." Paul Collingwood

SEASON

Jaws

31 JULY: There was a nationwide stir when amateur angler Kevin Keeble published a picture of a Great White shark in the *Newquay Guardian*. National newspapers picked up the story, with the *Sun* offering readers a free Jaws ring tone, and there was much debate about the safety of Cornish waters. Anxieties were allayed when Mr Keeble, a 52-year-old nightclub bouncer, admitted that the photo was a hoax, taken on a fishing trip near Cape Town, South Africa.

> "I didn't expect anyone to
> be daft enough to take it seriously."
> Kevin Keeble

Lord Lucan?

9 AUGUST: Roger Woodgate, a Briton living in New Zealand, was accused of being the missing Lord Lucan. A neighbour saw a picture of Lucan in a magazine and was convinced that it was Woodgate, a homeless ex-pat, who lives with his pet possum in a Land Rover in Marton on the North Island. Woodgate pointed out that he is younger and shorter than the disgraced peer. There have been over 70 'sightings' of Lucan worldwide since he vanished in 1974.

> "I wouldn't be surprised to learn
> he is Lucan. There's quite a
> resemblance."
> Bob Buchanan, local mayor

PEOPLE IN

"you never know when you might need a facial"

"the American people are proud to welcome Your Majesty"

THE NEWS

"I'm off to do the biggest show of my life"

"I feel 80 per cent of my life is completely normal"

7 May:
President Bush welcomed HM The Queen to the White House and aged her by 200 years.

"The American people are proud to welcome Your Majesty back to the United States, a nation you've come to know very well.

After all, you've dined with ten US presidents. You helped our nation celebrate its bicentennial in 17... – in 1976."

Profile: J K Rowling

Best-selling author, global brand, benefactor and mother

Following the success of her seventh and final Harry Potter book in 2007, which sold a record 11 million copies in its first 24 hours worldwide, J K Rowling is looking forward to spending more time with her family.

J K Rowling, who began her literary career as a single mother, scribbling in restaurants with a baby at her elbow, is now said to be worth about £545 million, the 13th richest woman in the UK.

Now that the seventh and final book in the series is complete, Rowling is working on two new books, one for children and one for adults. She is also planning an 'encyclopaedia' of the wizarding world consisting of various unpublished material and notes. Profits from this work will go to charity – she makes substantial contributions to charities that combat poverty and social inequality and support children, single parent families and multiple sclerosis research.

Named Joanne Rowling, she was advised to acquire the ambiguous initials by her publishers, who feared that young boys might be reluctant to buy books written by a female author.

"I feel 80 per cent of my life is completely normal. It involves me raising my children, going to the supermarket and just living normally. My husband and I both work. Ten per cent is fabulous in that you get invited to a Harry Potter premiere and you have a lot of fun at it. And 10 per cent is the downside when you have tabloid journalists banging on your relatives' doors offering them money for their stories."
J K Rowling

THE STORY OF J K ROWLING

1965 JKR born, Gloucestershire

1970 JKR writes a short story, *Rabbit*

1983 At the University of Exeter she reads for a BA in French and Classics

1986 JKR works as a researcher/bilingual secretary for Amnesty International

1990 on a train trip from Manchester to London, she develops the idea for a story of a boy attending a school of wizardry

1992 JKR moves to Porto, Portugal to teach English as a foreign language. She marries a Portuguese television journalist

1993 Jessica Isabel Rowling Arantes born

1993 JKR separates from first husband

1994 JKR and daughter move to Edinburgh

1995 JKR completes the manuscript for *Harry Potter and the Philosopher's Stone* on an old manual typewriter

1997 Bloomsbury publishes *Philosopher's Stone*, but advises JKR to get a day job, warning her that she has little chance of making money in children's books

1998–2007 JKR writes a further six Harry Potter books, selling over 325 million in all

2001 JKR marries Neil Murray, an anaesthesiologist, at her Aberfeldy home

2003 David Gordon Rowling Murray born

2005 Mackenzie Jean Rowling Murray born

2007 *Harry Potter and the Deathly Hallows*, the seventh and final book of the series, is the fastest-selling book of all time

RECORD BREAKERS

TAKING IT TO THE LIMIT

3 January: Michael Perham, 14, became the youngest ever person to sail the Atlantic single-handed.

"I was never really that frightened... You are away from your friends and family. You're almost totally isolated. That does get to you." Michael Perham

15 July: Lewis Pugh became the first man to swim at the geographic North Pole.

"I can't think of a better way to show that climate change is a reality than by swimming in a place that should be totally frozen over." Lewis Pugh

Michael set sail from Gibraltar on 18 November 2006.
He stopped briefly in the Canaries & Cape Verde
Islands for equipment repairs, then headed west for
the Caribbean. After six weeks at sea, battling rough
waters and gale-force winds, he sailed into English
Harbour, Antigua, escorted by a flotilla of boats.

Throughout Michael's 3,500-mile voyage his 28-foot
yacht, Cheeky Monkey, was shadowed by his father,
an experienced Yachtmaster. Both sailed in Tide 28
yachts, modified and equipped to bring them up to
ocean standards.

Michael, who started sailing at the age of seven, was
inspired to attempt the Atlantic voyage by Seb
Clover's record of 2003. Seb was 15 when he made
the crossing.

Michael Perham sails into English Harbour, Antigua

Lewis Pugh swam a kilometre in temperatures of
−1.8°C (28.8°F), the coldest water in which a human
has ever swum, in just swimming trunks and a cap.
It took 18 minutes and 50 seconds and Pugh declared
it "the hardest swim of my life".

Pugh, explorer and endurance swimmer, completed
this life-threatening swim to highlight how global
warming has melted the Artic ice-cap. Pugh,
Ambassador for WWF UK, hoped that it would
inspire world leaders to take climate change seriously.

He has a rare ability to withstand incredibly cold
temperatures. He says it's because he can increase his
core body temperature simply through concentrating.
Even so, he was in severe pain and admitted that he
very nearly quit.

Lewis Pugh swims in Arctic waters

PEDAL POWER

6 October: Jason Lewis completed the first ever human-powered circumnavigation of the globe, crossing the Greenwich meridian 13 years, 2 months and 24 days after he began his 46,000-mile journey.

Jason Lewis, then 26, set off from Greenwich on 12 June 1994 in his pedal-powered 26-foot boat, Moksha. He crossed the Channel twice, as well as the Atlantic, Pacific and Indian Oceans and the Timor Sea. He also used an assortment of mountain bikes, kayaks and roller blades to carry him across the world's continents.

During his epic journey he was chased by a crocodile in Australia, arrested as a spy in Egypt, broke both his legs, and suffered a potentially fatal case of blood poisoning, contracted 1,300 miles from land in the middle of the Pacific Ocean.

"It doesn't seem too different. I've had my first greasy spoon breakfast and the fried eggs taste the same... the weather hasn't changed and there are more speed cameras."

AN EPIC JOURNEY

July 1994: Lewis and expedition founder Steve Smith set out to pedal across the Channel to Lagos, Portugal.

Feb 1995: The pair complete their crossing of the Atlantic.

Sept 1996: Lewis completes his crossing of the USA by roller blade. Both legs are broken when he is hit by a drunk driver.

Sept 1997: Lewis and Smith cycle to Peru for a Pacific launch, but abort their mission because of adverse currents.

Sept 1998: Lewis and Smith set off from San Francisco. After Hawaii Lewis travels in stages alone and with other companions.

Aug 2000: Lewis becomes the first person to pedal the Pacific – 178 days.

2001: Lewis cycles 3,200 miles through Australia.

2005: Lewis mountain bikes and kayaks from Darwin through Indonesia to Singapore.

2006: Lewis bikes and walks from Singapore to Mumbai.

Jan 2007: Lewis pedals Moksha from Mumbai to the Horn of Africa. From here he kayaks and mountain bikes to Istanbul, Turkey.

April 2007: Lewis mountain bikes through Europe.

Sept 2007: He arrives in Ostend, ready to make a Channel crossing on Moksha.

Oct 2007: Lewis pedals up the Thames and pushes Moksha over the Greenwich meridian.

A PRINCESS REMEMBERED

Princess Diana died, aged 36, along with her companion Dodi Al Fayed, 42, on 31 August 1997. Her death provoked an unprecedented outpouring of national grief. On the tenth anniversary of her death, admirers of the late princess tied flowers and cards to the gates of Kensington Palace – her London residence – as they did in 1997. An inquest into her death was launched on 2 October.

Testino and the National Portrait Gallery

Representing the princess's life in images proved to be a popular and fitting way to remember her multi-faceted and influential persona: from the shy teenager, to the glamorous and sophisticated style icon, to the tireless campaigner for charities.

1 July: An exhibition of pictures taken by acclaimed photographer Mario Testino – including many pictures not previously shown in public – opened at Diana's London home, Kensington Palace.

14 July: The National Portrait Gallery brought together a diverse range of portraits of the princess from its own Collection, by photographers including Lord Snowdon, David Bailey and Mario Testino. The display covered the years from her engagement to the Prince of Wales in 1981, to her last public charitable campaign in 1997.

31 August: Memorial Day

A service of memorial was held at the Guards Chapel near Buckingham Palace. The Queen, Prince Philip, Prince Charles, and the princess's sons, William and Harry all attended. Others present included Prime Minister Gordon Brown and his predecessors Tony Blair and John Major. Camilla, the Duchess of Cornwall, was invited to the hour-long memorial but on 27 August she announced she would not be attending, saying her presence would be a distraction.

Services were held at churches around the country, including Bristol Cathedral, Manchester Cathedral and Llandaff Cathedral, Cardiff. A service was also held at St Mary's Church, in Great Brington, near Althorp, Diana's final resting place. It was the first time Althorp had been opened on an anniversary of her death.

At 11 a.m. the owner of Harrods, Mohamed Al Fayed, whose son Dodi died in the crash alongside the princess, laid flowers at a shrine he has built at the London store and held a two-minute silence.

"She made us and so many other people happy... When she was alive we completely took for granted her unrivalled love of life, laughter, fun and folly."

Prince Harry

VICTORIA IN THE USA

2007 saw Victoria Beckham take America by storm as she accompanied her husband to LA where he plays for American soccer team, the LA Galaxy.

THE RISE OF VICTORIA BECKHAM

1974 VB born in Hertfordshire

1982–91 VB at Jason Theatre School

1992 VB at Laine Arts Theatre College, Surrey

1995 VB answers ad in *Stage* looking for five girls who can sing and dance. The Spice Girls are born

1996 *Wannabe* goes straight to No. 1

1997 *Spiceworld the Movie* launches

1997 VB meets future husband David Beckham

1998 Geri Halliwell quits Spice Girls

1999 Brooklyn Beckham born

1999 VB & David Beckham marry

2001 Spice Girls disbands

2001 Victoria releases solo single, *Not Such An Innocent Girl*, and a self-titled debut album

2002 Romeo Beckham born

2003 Another brief foray into music, teaming up with US hip hop artist Damian Dash

2004 'This Groove/Let Your Head Go' reaches No. 3 in the UK charts, but VB wants to focus on her family

2005 Cruz Beckham born

2006 VB's Rock and Republic jeans sell out across UK

2006 Victoria's book *That Extra Half Inch* is published

2007 dVb is launched: jeans, handbags and sunglasses

2007 The Beckhams move to Los Angeles

"I think people are really going to see me for the first time... I think they have this impression that I'm this miserable cow who doesn't smile. But I'm actually quite the opposite. When you're out there, they're trying to get pictures up your shirt, down your top... With all the flashes, it's as much as you can do to just find your car. I'm going to try and smile more for America." Victoria Beckham

"I have been busy having a good look around LA, checking out the restaurants and the beauty parlours – well you never know when you might need a facial!" Victoria Beckham

May: Victoria's driving skills came to the attention of the LAPD. She was pulled over for making an illegal turn and ordered to apply for a California driver's licence. The episode was caught on TV cameras and many claim it was a publicity stunt. Victoria was not phased: "The policeman was gorgeous. And he loved my shoes."

June: dVb, her own label denim collection, launched in New York. The two back pocket designs – a star and the dVb signature – were strategically placed to flatter a woman's curves. She even had Jennifer Lopez road test a pair to make sure they suited curvier girls. VB said: "I'm a real consumer, and I think I know how real women want to look."

January: Madame Tussauds in New York marked the arrival of the Beckhams with a special exhibit of President Bush holding a sign welcoming the couple to America.

Victoria has been working hard, especially on the Los Angeles social scene. She and David have made many friends in high places – new acquaintances famously include Tom Cruise and Katie Holmes.

July: the LA home, a $22 million Beverly Hills Mediterranean-style villa, is a 13,000-square-foot, six-bedroom house, with tennis court and pool. In an interview with W magazine, Victoria said: "We didn't want anything too huge, too fancy, too ostentatious." She said this house offered "something quite practical for the kids. It's a light, happy house, with a great corridor the kids are going to love when they are roller-skating."

1 July:
David Beckham joins the Los Angeles Galaxy and Major League Soccer in the US

"I look forward to the new challenge of growing the world's most popular game in a country that is as passionate about its sport as my own." David Beckham

SUMMER 2007
BECKHAM
COMES TO AMERICA
BE A PART OF HISTORY
LAGALAXY.COM
1.877.3GALAXY

MEN BEHAVING BADLY

Fredalo

18 MARCH: England cricketer Andrew Flintoff was sacked as the team's vice-captain and banned from playing in a match against Canada after a bout of drinking led to an accident involving a pedalo in St Lucia. He was rescued after falling into the sea and getting into difficulties. Flintoff publicly apologised.

5 JUNE: Team captain Michael Vaughan sparked fresh controversy when he appeared to blame Flintoff's drunken antics for England's failure in the Caribbean: "You have to be honest: the 'Fredalo' incident did affect the team. It did affect morale."

"I know what I did was completely wrong and I have to take full responsibility for it. There can be no excuses on my part." Andrew Flintoff

Currygate

13 MAY: *Who Wants to be a Millionaire?* host Chris Tarrant was arrested for alleged assault. The incident took place in a Nottingham curry house when Tarrant allegedly lobbed some cutlery at the table of a couple with whom he'd been chatting. The man complained to the police that the fork Tarrant had thrown cut his arm, and Tarrant was arrested and cautioned. He was released on bail after several hours in a cell.

Tarrant has found himself under close media scrutiny after the collapse of his marriage in 2006. The incident in the curry house hit the headlines the following day.

"It was just a bit of horseplay... There was no malice involved at all."
Chris Tarrant

Wham-Bam!

Get Out of Jail Free

26 FEBRUARY: Singer George Michael was spotted slumped at the wheel of his car in the early hours of the morning near Hyde Park Corner. Police searched him and found he was in possession of Class C drugs. In March he accepted a police caution for being in possession of cannabis.

8 MAY: Michael appeared in court on charges relating to an earlier incident in October 2006 when he was arrested after his car obstructed traffic lights in north London. He pleaded guilty to a charge of driving while unfit through drugs.

8 JUNE: The day before he was due to appear at Wembley Stadium, he was sentenced to 100 hours of community service and banned from driving for two years.

> "I'm glad to put this behind me... now I'm off to do the biggest show of my life." George Michael

FEBRUARY: Charged with four driving offences.
MAY: Stopped/searched by police on Kensington High Street and charged with a series of driving and drugs offences. Doherty pleaded guilty to possession of Class A drugs (ketamine, crack, heroin) and cannabis.
JULY: Avoided jail when judge deferred sentencing to give him an opportunity to clean up and go to rehab.
AUGUST: Turned up late at court for sentencing but proceedings were adjourned for pre-sentence reports until September. Banished from London for a month. He was subsequently arrested in Tower Hamlets, East London at 2 a.m. on suspicion of possession of drugs and breaching bail conditions. He was released without charge from West London Magistrates' Court following a legal technicality. Accusations appeared in the tabloids that Doherty's kitten had cocaine in its blood system.
SEPTEMBER: Checked into rehab for a five-week stint.
OCTOBER: Due to face sentencing on 26 October for driving illegally while in possession of a number of drugs, including heroin and crack cocaine.

WAG WEDDINGS

15–16 June: Four lavish footballers' weddings in one weekend; a fortnight later 'WAG' entered the *Oxford English Dictionary*

JOHN TERRY & TONI POOLE

WHEN 15 June

WHERE Blenheim Palace, Woodstock, Oxfordshire

COST Rumoured to be £500–£800k

ENTERTAINMENT Lionel Richie

GUESTS included Frank Lampard, Ashley and Cheryl Cole, Jamie and Louise Redknapp and Chelsea owner Roman Abramovich

MAGAZINE *OK!* reportedly paid £1 million

GARY NEVILLE & EMMA HADFIELD

WHEN 16 June

WHERE Manchester Cathedral followed by their multi-million pound mansion

COST Rumoured to be £1 million

ENTERTAINMENT Jon Cristos

THE DRESS Amanda Wakeley

GUESTS Wayne Rooney and Coleen McLoughlin flew by helicopter from Steven Gerrard's wedding

"My life is nothing like the Footballers' Wives on TV. It's not all celebrity parties and trendy clubs." Alex Curran

"I've been with Toni since I was 18 and she was on more money than me... She used to take me for dinner." John Terry

STEVEN GERRARD & ALEX CURRAN

WHEN 16 June

WHERE Cliveden House Hotel, Berkshire

COST Rumoured to be £500k–£1 million

ENTERTAINMENT Gary Barlow

GUESTS included Michael Owen, Robbie Fowler, Ashley Cole and Cheryl Tweedy, Wayne Rooney and Coleen McLoughlin

MAGAZINE *OK!* reportedly paid £800k

MICHAEL CARRICK & LISA ROUGHEAD

WHEN 16 June

WHERE St Peter's Church, nr Melton Mowbray, and Stapleford Park, Leicestershire

COST Rumoured to be a modest £250k

THE DRESS Christan Lacroix

GUESTS included Joe Cole, fiancée Carly Zucker and Jermain Defoe

MAGAZINE *Hello!* reportedly paid £200k

I THEE WED...

Elizabeth Hurley's weddings caused a media storm both in the UK and in India.

On 3 March, Liz Hurley married Indian businessman Arun Nayar at Sudeley Castle, Gloucestershire. Three hundred guests attended the lavish event, which was exclusively covered by *Hello!* in a deal reportedly worth £2 million. The couple then jetted off to India to continue the celebrations for nearly a week before they were married again in a traditional Indian ceremony at the Umaidh Bhawan in Jodhpur.

The couple's celebrations hit the press a month later, when Nayar's father publicly disowned the couple, claiming that they had humiliated him and his family at the wedding. Furthermore, a legal complaint was filed in India, claiming that they had broken Hindu tradition by indulging in public displays of affection and drinking before the ceremony.

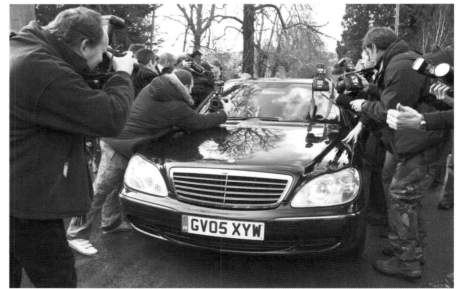

Guests arrive at Sudeley Castle

IT'S ALL OVER...

Celebrity divorces in 2007: acrimony, alimony and a little good will…

PAUL McCARTNEY AND HEATHER MILLS

Four-year marriage, with one child

Heather apparently ordered London-based Mishcon de Reya to fight Sir Paul for £200 million.

The couple announced plans to split in May 2006. On 23 January 2007 Ms Mills' lawyers denied that she had agreed a financial settlement with McCartney. They appeared in the High Court for the first stage of their divorce hearing on 1 March.

Sir Paul is worth around £800 million. The settlement represents a sizeable chunk of his fortune.

On 12 October court negotiations over the settlement broke down and were adjourned until a public hearing in February 2008.

> "One of the most high-profile marriage breakdowns in history…"
> The Times

CHRIS EVANS AND BILLIE PIPER

Three-year marriage

In June the *decree nisi* was processed in London's High Court. It cited two years' separation with consent/irreconcilable differences.

There was no bitter wrangling. Billie did not want to take any of her husband's £30 million fortune.

ROMAN ABRAMOVICH AND IRINA

15-year marriage, with five children

A Russian divorce was finalised at the end of February.

It is not known what share of her husband's £11 billion fortune 39-year-old Irina has won but it may have cost the multi-billionaire upwards of £1 billion.

SALMAN RUSHDIE AND PADMA LAKSHMI

Three-year marriage

Rushdie's fourth divorce came a couple of weeks after he was knighted by the Queen.

The couple's age difference is considerable – Padma is 36 and Salman is 60.

A statement from the author's agent in New York said: "Salman Rushdie has agreed to divorce his wife Padma Lakshmi because of her desire to end their marriage."

BABY TALK

Public attention focused on a celebrity baby boom in 2007. Famous parents and their offspring have also acted as a stimulus for a baby shopping bonanza.

Princess Tiàamii

Parents: 29-year-old glamour model, Katie Price (aka Jordan) and former Australian pop star, Peter Andre

When: 29 June

Weight: 6lb 13oz

Fact: The couple also have a son, Junior, while Jordan has another son, Harvey, from a previous relationship with footballer Dwight Yorke

"Princess because she is our princess and Tiàamii was Pete's idea because it's taken from our mums' names, Pete's mum Thea and mine, Amy… We've put an accent over the first 'a' to make it a bit more exotic and two 'ii's at the end just to make it a bit different."
Katie Price

Ava Bailey

Parents: Myleene Klass and fiancé Graham Quinn (they got together in 2001 when Quinn worked as a bodyguard for Hear'Say)

When: 16 August

Weight: 5lb 9oz

Fact: Ava was born three-and-a-half weeks early

Beau

Parents: Baby Spice Emma Bunton and Jade Jones, who have been together for eight years

When: 10 August

Weight: 7lb 15oz

Other: Beau was born at London's Portland Hospital. Emma requested Coca-Cola and flapjacks afterwards

Angel Iris

Parents: Mel B and Eddie Murphy

When: 3 April

Weight: 5lb 4oz

Fact: Angel is Murphy's seventh child (or sixth – sources differ!) and Melanie's second. DNA tests were needed to confirm that Murphy is the father after he denied it

Heidi Elizabeth

Parents: Kerry Katona and Mark Croft

When: 20 February

Weight: 5lb

Fact: Heidi is Kerry's third child. She has two daughters from her marriage to Brian McFadden: Molly, five, and Lily Sue, three

Grace

Parents: Former tennis star Tim Henman and wife Lucy

When: 14 September

Weight: 8lb 11oz

Other: Baby Grace is Tim and Lucy's third daughter; they already have Rosie, born in 2002, and Olivia, born in 2004

Donovan Rory

Parents: Sara MacDonald and Noel Gallagher

When: 22 September

Weight: 7lb 5oz

Fact: Born at London's private Portland Hospital. Donovan is a step-brother for Noel's daughter Anais, seven, with Meg Mathews

Ruby Megan

Parents: Charlotte Church and Gavin Henson

When: 20 September

Weight: 6lb 12oz (exactly the same weight as Charlotte when she was born)

Fact: Ruby was born at the couple's £800,000 home in Wales

SHOWBIZ

"Am I mad, in a coma, or back in time?"

"I can say that Jade is not a bad person"

AND MEDIA

"I think you fell in love with her, not with me"

"I want to hear laughter, I want to see people fight"

SEARCHING FOR THE SOUND OF MUSIC

Andrew Lloyd Webber on bringing musical theatre back to the people...

It started when Scarlett Johansson turned me down. Or at least her people did. But before I reveal all I must backtrack...

When I was a kid I was a huge fan of Richard Rodgers. These days if I say I love Richard Rodgers' tunes, people think I am talking about an architect. But back in 1961 the name Richard Rodgers was synonymous with the legendary Rodgers & Hammerstein of which Rodgers was the composing half. I wrote a fan letter to Rodgers and astoundingly he replied. He asked me to a rehearsal of the new Rodgers & Hammerstein show to hit London – *The Sound of Music*.

Thus a gauche, very serious schoolboy got to the first night of a show that was destined to be the longest running American musical in London of its time. It opened to appalling reviews. I remember what the boys at my school taunted me with when I swaggered in to the school common room the morning after my first invitation to an opening night. "Look at this one Lloydy. It says if you're a diabetic craving sweet things take along a load of insulin and you will not fail to thrill to *The Sound of Music*".

"*YOU WILL NOT FAIL TO THRILL TO THE SOUND OF MUSIC*" was the big quote outside the Palace Theatre for seven years. At least I learned from that first night the art of creative misuse of reviews. Yet among all the diatribes, a few critics recognised how great the tunes were. Most scribes wondered why Rodgers & Hammerstein – who had dared to take on racial issues in 1949 with *South Pacific* and redefined musical theatre with *Oklahoma!* six years previously – had sold out to what everyone thought was a saccharine story.

I didn't think they had. I thought even then that the reason why *The Sound of Music* was critically mauled was because the heroine, Maria, was miscast. When *The Sound of Music* opened on Broadway it starred the 50-ish Mary Martin as Maria. She was a legendary Broadway star. But brilliant as she clearly was, she didn't exactly fit the bill as a girl who 'climbs a tree and scrapes her knee'.

So when I first saw *The Sound of Music* in London, I loved the music, the Maria was great, but I did not believe she was a girl who was a tomboy. Surely the Rodgers & Hammerstein 'danger element' comes from a story where a young girl finds herself in a household of seven kids, the oldest of whom is only sixteen going on seventeen. She then captivates the children's martinet father in front of their very eyes. If you cast Maria as only a very few years older than 16-year-old Liesl, you have a story that starts to press a red button or two. That's why I asked Miss Johansson if she would play Maria for me at the London Palladium. For here was a brilliantly talented young actress of exactly the right age. And I knew something else. Scarlett can sing.

> "If I couldn't have a real 20-year-old star as my Maria I would have to create one. Maybe TV could do this for me."

When her people said no, I had a problem. My co-producer David Ian owned the British rights to *The Sound of Music*. He quite rightly balked at co-producing an old show with no star name in the role, particularly in the huge London Palladium. Older star names than Scarlett were bandied about. But that didn't interest me. I wanted to produce *The Sound of Music* with a young Maria. David understandably was on the verge of withdrawing. *The Sound of Music* with a young Maria looked dead in the water.

I don't know what side of the bed I got out of with the words 'reality TV casting'. If I couldn't have a real 20-year-old star as my Maria I would have to create one. Maybe TV could do this for me.

I knew from recent auditioning experiences that there were talented young unknown actresses out there who could play Maria, but none of them could sell a ticket. What, I figured, would happen if I could persuade a TV network to make programme to feature these girls and find my star? Might I not create a star, but also provide a showcase for kids who never would get the break TV can provide, even if they didn't win? But I knew that if I failed in my quest, my whole career would be questioned.

It was obvious that for a programme of this sort I had to talk to the BBC. My mantra was 'We nurture, not torture'. With the BBC, I was under no pressure to audition talentless wannabees in order to provide slagging off soundbites. Further, my producers at the BBC understood that you can't 'reality cast' most musicals. You have to find a show that a wide audience knows, therefore has an opinion about, and can share in the experience.

It would be stretching optimism to the limit to say that when the BBC first nervously screened *How Do You Solve A Problem Like Maria?* in the notoriously difficult August Saturday evening slot that anyone believed we had a programme whose final's viewing figures would take on *X Factor*.

So why did it work? Hindsight is a great thing. You normally want it when you've made a catastrophic mistake. Casting a show by television could so easily have been disastrous. After all, the copycat programme to cast *Grease* failed on both sides of the Atlantic, even when produced in the UK by Simon Cowell.

But *How Do You Solve a Problem Like Maria?* and its sibling *Any Dream Will Do* worked a treat. Not only did the programmes bring very talented young artists into everyone's front rooms, but they brought musical theatre back to the people. Coupled with that other international phenomenon, Disney's *High School Musical*, there's no question that a huge new audience is embracing musical theatre, even if in the latter case it's somewhat pubescent.

Apart from my personal jeopardy, even more terrifying was that my task was to persuade a Saturday night TV audience that I wasn't looking for a Julie Andrews clone. What I was not prepared for were cries of anguish from the theatre profession ranging from the actors' union Equity to Sir Trevor Nunn. They claimed that the TV casting process was demeaning to actors. It could have been, but I produced my 'nurture not torture' mantra. There was month when I thought I would be chucked out of the Society of London Theatre!

To be frank, I don't know whether TV casting for a musical can happen very often. Sure as day leads to night, there will be many attempts, but, as I have already said, I believe that 'reality TV' works for only a tiny number of shows, shows like *The Sound of Music* that a TV audience knows and has a real opinion on when it comes to casting the central role.

However at least my activities in the summer of 2006 and 2007 threw the theatre old guard into a delicious furore of sixes and sevens.

CURTAIN UP

27 February: Daniel Radcliffe, who plays the young wizard in the Harry Potter films, made his stage debut in Peter Schaffer's *Equus* at the Gielgud Theatre.

Critics praised Radcliffe for his confident performance, a sustained theatrical tour de force, as 17-year-old Alan Strang, a boy who inexplicably blinds six horses with a metal spike. Radcliffe found himself under fierce scrutiny when it was announced that he would appear nude on stage, a risqué step that may jeopardise his future relations with the producers of the lucrative Harry Potter films.

Born in 1989, Racliffe first played Harry Potter in 2001, and has starred in five film adaptations – *Harry Potter and the Order of the Phoenix* premiered on 3 July 2007. The stage rookie is a seasoned Hollywood performer – on 9 July he left imprints of his hands and feet (and wand) outside Grauman's Chinese Theater.

"There's never enough time to do nothing!"
Daniel Radcliffe

FINAL CALL

8 June: Darcy Bussell's final performance as principal ballerina, in MacMillan's *Song of the Earth* at Covent Garden, marked the end of an era.

Bussell had chosen to exit on a high note, at the peak of her career, so that she could spend more time with her two young daughters. Her performance was met with a long and heartfelt standing ovation; she made her final bow on a stage buried under flowers.

Bussell was born in London in 1969. She did not begin to study ballet seriously until she was 13, when she enrolled in the Royal Ballet School. In 1987 she joined the Sadler's Wells Royal Ballet, and moved on to the Royal Ballet in 1988 where her talent was spotted by the choreographer Keith MacMillan, who gave her a leading role in *The Prince of Pagodas*.

A year later, in 1989, she was made Principal, at the time the youngest ballerina to be given this honour. Her many roles have spanned the classical repertoire – from *Sleeping Beauty* to *The Nutcracker* and *Giselle*. She also proved a hit in postmodernist pieces by William Forsythe and Twyla Tharp.

"Being a mother has made my life complete."

Darcy Bussell

"It may have seemed like it was bad, but I can say that Jade is not a bad person, she's just young." Shilpa Shetty

"I will not justify my actions, because I'm wrong, I know I'm wrong." Jade Goody

SHILPA *v* JADE

January: *Celebrity BB5* captured the world's attention over allegations of racism in the Big Brother house.

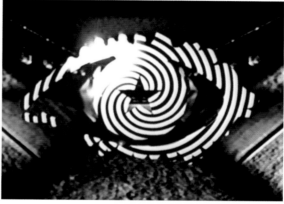

One is a sophisticated Bollywood beauty with millions of fans, who speaks six languages and is a black belt in karate. The other is a loud-mouthed Bermondsey lass whose only claim to fame was coming fourth in *Big Brother 3*. Only one programme could bring these opposites together.

Shilpa Shetty came to London to represent Indians on *Celebrity Big Brother 5* as glamorous, modern and cosmopolitan, but her housemates couldn't even be bothered to learn her name. Famously, Jade Goody referred to her as 'Shilpa Poppadom'.

Fellow-housemates Danielle Lloyd (model and former girlfriend of Teddy Sheringham) and Jo O'Meara (of S Club Seven) also helped to make Shilpa's 26-day ordeal "the most mortifying experience of my life".

International Outcry

The debacle certainly angered many people. Ofcom, the UK media regulator, received over 40,000 complaints, and Carphone Warehouse cancelled its £3 million sponsorship deal. In India, protestors burnt Goody's effigy in the streets of Patna and government members complained to Gordon Brown, who was on an official visit.

Shilpa, the eventual winner, believed that Jade's behaviour stemmed from jealousy and insecurity. A remorseful Jade pledged profits from the show to charity, and made a 'private visit' to India.

On 24 August Channel 4, accused by Ofcom of "serious editorial misjudgments", announced that they would not be screening *Celebrity BB* next year.

WHAT KATIE DID:
THE REALITY OF REALITY TV

by Katie Hopkins

"You're in" said the producer over the phone, confirming my place in *The Apprentice 2007*.

"Hell's Bells" I thought.

"You're in" said Sir Alan across the boardroom table, confirming my place in the final.

"Hell's Bells" I thought.

"You're on the front cover, naked, having sex with your boyfriend in a field" said my boss. And finally the alarm bells went off.

For the next 30 minutes I scrambled to call the people who could help get me out of this mess. My partner (married), my agent (marvellous), my boss (mad).

The next morning at seven I drove to my local garage wearing sunglasses three times the size of my head, aware that I was probably being followed, and acutely aware that I was up to my neck in it. There, on the forecourt, were pictures of me. Naked. In a field.

With reality TV, if you become the 'undisputed star of the show' it is not the TV show that is problematic in itself, it is the simple fact that everyone wants to know about your 'real' life. The reality of reality TV is that it extends, tentacle-like, into your private world. It is pervasive and permeating and takes no prisoners. Your real life is actually the reality that everyone wants to hear about. And so it was with me.

And my reality is that there are more skeletons in my closet than the Natural History Museum. At 32 I have had a colourful life. Before the show was due to hit the air, we had scheduled briefings with the PR agents handling us.

When I attended my session I kept all my little secrets close to my chest. I figured the fewer people that knew about my private life, the better. And after all, it was only *The Apprentice* and I was just one of 16 others. I was about as wrong as grown men in scout uniform.

Rapidly, I became 'the most hated woman in Britain' and the nation's scarlet woman. I also earned the label of posh totty and superbitch. None of which seemed compatible with the truth of me; an intelligent working mother of two with a natty line in put-downs.

> "Reality TV works on an inverse relationship. The more you want from fame, the less you get. The less you expect, the quicker you are propelled into the spotlight."

Discrepancy between perception and reality is a common theme. For example, all the Apprentices have experienced very different realities from the same show. For some, *The Apprentice* has changed their lives very little, delivering nothing at all, even when expectations were very great. For others, there have been varying degrees of reward or notoriety.

It seems that reality TV works on an inverse relationship. The more you want from fame, the less you get. The less you expect, the quicker you are propelled into the spotlight. Thinking back, this was representative of the interview and audition stage. I filled in my application form in 15 minutes, in my bikini in my garden in the sunshine; I breezed through the audition with an equally sunny disposition.

Conversely, the majority of the people I chatted to during those days should have been sectioned. I would have locked them up for the amount of preparation they had done – like contacting other *Apprentice* contestants for advice. Some of them even knew the format of each task on the show. I wouldn't want to share a wing at Wandsworth with them, let alone a house in Notting Hill.

Being allowed into our accommodation for the first time, the rest of the Apprentices 'whooped' and 'yeehaa'd' their exploratory way around the house in a festival of noise and over-excitement. I realised rapidly that a house with three bedrooms was never going to accommodate 16 people any better than an NHS mixed mental ward without the curtains.

Fellow contestants Simon Ambrose and Kristina Grimes

As a home-owning 32-year-old, with a partner and two children, it was back to boarding school; bunk beds, shared showers and no wardrobes to speak of. Washing was laundered for us by the housemistress and the telephone was out of bounds. However, for those of us still in short shorts it was a great extension of an old lifestyle – constant company and a life free of the worries and responsibilities of the real world.

The filming of *The Apprentice* is rather like one of those movies where the character wakes up after an horrific accident only to discover that their identity has been stolen. You have no credit card, no phone, no bedroom to call your own, no computer, no internet, no access to the outside world and no privacy.

According to Margaret Atwood, there are two types of freedom, freedom to and freedom from. *The Apprentice* certainly gave you freedom from the nauseating minutiae that pollute our daily lives – shopping, telephone calls, post, bills, car parking, buying fuel etc.

> I do not apologise for anything I have done. I am proud of what I achieved.

However, it is also stellar in its ability to make you understand the value of freedom to. You yearn for the freedom to step outside the front door. For the freedom to take a pee on your own. For the freedom to have a blazing row and not be asked by a producer to talk to camera about how you felt about it. Pope John Paul II denounced reality TV as incompatible with human dignity, and he had a point. I don't think you have to sacrifice your dignity to appear on these shows, but I think there is plenty of opportunity for you to do so if you wish.

The parallel of reality TV to pantomime season on the pier is not unreasonable. There are the actors, booked in advance, picked to play certain parts. There are the costumes, my 'white suit' worn repeatedly as a short cut for the audience to understand my character, and there are the scenes themselves, ingeniously constructed by the real stars of the show; the production team. In this year's Apprentice pantomime, 'Cinderella Simon', Lohit was the fairy prince, and Tre played a superb 'Buttons', keeping Simon out of trouble. And I, with my brutal honesty, got to play the wicked stepmother, the villain of the show. A role I did not contrive, I certainly did not prepare the script for, but one I played out rather well.

In a world of immediacy, reality TV can surely deliver. It acts like a massive compressor machine, squashing time, emotions, feelings, actions and reactions into an ever-tighter space. And this is consistent across a number of formats; Jordan managed to fall in love with her future husband in the jungle; Paul Burrell managed to redeem his public persona. Yet, as with anything compressed, something has to give.

And give it did. For Geri it was her emotions, giving way under the pressure of a task too far, for Jadine it was the memories of her daughter and missing her like a single mother would, for Rory it was a conflict with Tre. For others, the strain came after the show aired and the media frenzy began, particularly via internet forums. Sophie had to physically remove her ability to log in to stop reading the spiteful commentary. This stuff is like an internet road crash: you are compelled to read it and then horrified by what you have seen.

Protecting yourself is not easy. But I have learned a great deal from the experience. I have learned to cherish privacy and the intimacy of having secrets that the world doesn't know. I have learned the value of net curtains and a great agent. I have understood why you should never be face-on to the camera and why pink lipstick will never be a great idea. I have learned that old acquaintances with a story to tell will override their dignity for dirty money. And I have learned that wives never blame their husbands.

Some of these things I learned too late to save myself.

But I do not apologise for anything I have done. I am proud of what I achieved and happy that I have lived my life guided by my heart. If you didn't like what you read, don't read it. If you didn't like what you heard, don't listen and if you didn't like what you saw, sometimes neither did I.

We all have defining moments in life, moments that will change our world forever. Reality TV is a brilliant, exciting and exhilarating roller coaster. I recommend the ride to anyone. Just be aware that if the wind blows, people will be able to see that you are wearing no knickers.

AND THE WINNER IS...

Dragons' Den (BBC)

Dancing on Ice (ITV)

Series 4 February–March; Series 5 October–November.

The idea: entrepreneurs pitch their ideas to a panel of business heavyweights (the Dragons) to secure financial investment.

Host: Evan Davis, the BBC's economics editor.

Judges: 'The Dragons' – Duncan Bannatyne (health club guru), Peter Jones (communications giant), Theo Paphitis (retail magnate), Deborah Meaden (leisure/retail goddess), Richard Farleigh (series 4, Australian private investor), James Caan (series 5, venture capitalist/founder of Hamilton Bradshaw).

Fact: Series 4 featured a 'woolly warmer' – a bag designed to solve the nightmare of how to keep lambs cosy, and an egg-boiler that didn't boil eggs.

Winners: include Levi Roots (real name Keith), who was backed to the tune of £50,000 to produce his Reggae Reggae sauce, which went on to sell almost 500,000 bottles in its first three months on the shelves of a major supermarket chain.

Final: 17 March.

The idea: eleven celebrities took to the ice with a professional skating partner. One couple was voted off each week after a 'skate-off'. The celebrities were put through their paces in training each week by pros including Jayne Torvill and Christopher Dean.

Hosts: Phillip Schofield and Holly Willoughby.

Judges: 'The Ice Panel' – Nicky Slater (Brit ice dancer), Natalia Bestemianova (Soviet figure skater), Jason Gardiner (choreographer/singer/theatre producer), Karen Barber (British ice dancer/former skating partner of Nicky Slater), Robin Cousins (British figure skater).

Winner: Kyran Bracken (rugby player), partnered by pro Melanie Lambert.

Fact: the show became a hit in Britain, with 13 million viewers tuning in to see the final. The concept didn't stop there – a Champion of Champions competition took place on 24 March, featuring finalists from both series. Again, Kyran Bracken left triumphant.

> "There are three reasons to be in business. To make money, to have fun – and to make money." Theo Paphitis, Dragon, *Dragons' Den*

Britain's Got Talent (ITV)

Final: 17 June.

The idea: search for Britain's 'best' amateur talent act.

Hosts: Ant & Dec.

Judges: Simon Cowell, Piers Morgan, Amanda Holden.

Winner: Carphone Warehouse employee Paul Potts who proved himself as an opera singer and picked up the £100,000 prize. His debut album *One Chance* claimed the Number One spot in the UK Album chart on 22 July.

Facts: Paul Potts met his wife in an internet chatroom. Drag act The Kit Kat Dolls were disqualified after the *News of the World* claimed that three of the group's members were prostitutes. Contestant Richard Bates disappeared from the show – he claimed that he quit after injuring himself in an accident involving his electric organ; the truth was that Lancashire Police had contacted producers to inform them that his name appears on the Sex Offenders Register following an offence committed in 2005.

Grease is the Word (ITV)

Final: 9 June.

The idea: search for unknowns to star as Sandy and Danny in the new London West End production of *Grease*. The show took the usual sing-to-be-eliminated format, first in couples, then as soloists.

Host: Zoë Ball.

Judges: David Ian (producer of the stage show), David Gest (lately famous for *I'm a Celebrity…*), Sinitta (80s pop star), Brian Friedman (American dance icon and *X Factor* judge).

Winners: Susan McFadden (24, a professional actress and singer) and Danny Bayne (19, student).

Interesting facts: Susan McFadden's big brother is former Westlife member Brian McFadden.

> "This feels amazing but it's going to be really weird performing every night and not having David Gest criticising me afterwards." winner Danny Bayne

"I want to see tears, I want to hear laughter, I want to see people fight, and I want to see people learn." Marco Pierre White

TOO MANY COOKS?

Britain's insatiable appetite for cooking programmes continued apace in 2007. Television audiences took masterclasses from the professionals, and enjoyed the spectacle of celebrities and wannabe kitchen stars being publicly humiliated by flamboyant media chefs.

Nigella Express

The domestic goddess returned to our screens in September, but the show was soon in the news after it was revealed that Nigella was using a studio kitchen, not her real London house, and that a bus journey she took was on a hired bus with extras. The BBC defended its actions after critics deemed the show a 'fake', saying, "this series is a factual entertainment cooking show, not an observational documentary, and it is perfectly normal procedure."

Hell's Kitchen

Marco Pierre White – famous for his ruthless temper – oversaw another collection of competing celebrities. Barry McGuigan beat *Emmerdale*'s Adele Silva in September's final, which attracted over six million viewers. The series hit the headlines when Lee Ryan walked out and Jim Davidson was asked to leave after making 'unacceptable remarks' to Brian Dowling.

F Word

Gordon Ramsay's series came under fire after misleading scenes. An episode showed the outspoken chef returning from a sea fishing trip with a good catch of sea bass. The fish had in fact been caught earlier that day by a spear-fishing expert. Channel 4 apologised, saying, "Regrettably, it appears that one part of the sea bass video-tape gave viewers an inaccurate impression about Gordon's involvement."

A TASTE OF THE REST

Jamie at Home: the naked chef showed the nation how to make the most of home grown, seasonal produce from the comfort of his Essex home.

The Restaurant: nine couples fought it out to run their own restaurant, complete with financial backing and support from top chef Raymond Blanc.

Kitchen Criminals: award-winning chefs John Burton Race and Angela Hartnett attempted to reform some of the country's worst cooks.

Great British Menu: Sat Bains, Richard Corrigan and Mark Hix fought off the competition in May to cook at a four-course banquet hosted by the British ambassador to France.

Celebrity MasterChef: Nadia Sawalha beat finalists Midge Ure and *Strictly Come Dancing* judge Craig Revel-Horwood to be crowned Celebrity MasterChef in June.

MasterChef Goes Large: winner Steve Wallis won the title of MasterChef in March.

Cook Yourself Thin: Harry, Gizzi, Sal and Sophie revealed how to drop a dress size and still eat cake...

Socks

BRITISH BROADCASTING CORPORAT

BBC

AUNTIE'S BLOOMERS

A series of high profile scandals at the BBC led to a massive loss of public confidence in 2007. In an attempt to assuage the public outcry, all BBC phone-ins were suspended at midnight on 19 July. High profile sackings and resignations followed as the BBC worked hard to regain the public's trust.

Faked phone-ins

Blue Peter had to apologise to viewers after the results of the 'Whose Shoes?' contest were faked in November 2006. When technical problems meant that viewers could not get through on a premium rate line, a researcher asked a child who was visiting the studio to 'phone in' and give her answer. The child's mother complained. On 10 July media watchdog Ofcom imposed a substantial £50,000 fine on the BBC for 'serious breaches' of the broadcasting code.

This was not the end of *Blue Peter*'s problems. On 24 September the BBC confirmed that staff had changed the results of an online poll to name its new cat. Voters had opted for the name 'Cookie', but staff decided to name the cat 'Socks'. The following day, an unprecedented step was taken when presenter Zoe Salmon, speaking on behalf of the programme, apologised on air. A new kitten was introduced and named Cookie. Richard Marson, the editor of *Blue Peter*, was sacked as a result of the scandal.

A misleading trailer

On 11 July a trailer was shown for an upcoming documentary, *A Year With The Queen*, which was made for the BBC by RDF Media. In the trailer the order of shots showing The Queen being photographed by Annie Leibovitz was changed so that it appeared as if she was storming out of the session, whereas she was in fact entering the room.

Peter Fincham, the controller of BBC One, told the press that it showed the monarch "losing it a bit and walking out in a huff". The story was picked up by the media, and the BBC was forced to apologise to Buckingham Palace and Annie Leibovitz the next day.

Former BBC executive Will Wyatt was commissioned to investigate and report on the incident. He said that it revealed "misjudgements, poor practice and ineffective systems". Following the publication of the report, on 5 October, Mr Fincham resigned.

Six other shows, including *Comic Relief*, *Children In Need* and radio shows *The Liz Kershaw Show* and *White Label* – all faked competition winners. *Saturday Kitchen* (10 Feb) encouraged viewers to phone in for a chance to appear on "next week's show", which was actually recorded just ten minutes later.

Not the only ones...

As phone-in scandals hit all the other main channels, they also found themselves in an unwelcome spotlight. On 8 March Five suspended all phone-ins when fictional winners were listed on screen after *Brainteaser*. On 26 September *GMTV* was fined an unprecedented £2 million for shortlisting potential winnners before phone lines closed. Richard and Judy (ITV) apologised on air when viewers were encouraged to enter the 'You Say, We Pay' quiz even after contestants had been chosen.

TIME TRAVELLERS

"The Doctor and Martha are destined to meet William Shakespeare, blood sucking alien Plasmavores, The Judoon – a clan of galactic stormtroopers – and a sinister intelligence at work in 1930s New York."

Russell T Davies, Executive Producer, *Doctor Who*

"My name is Sam Tyler. I had an accident and I woke up in 1973. Am I mad, in a coma, or back in time?"

Life on Mars

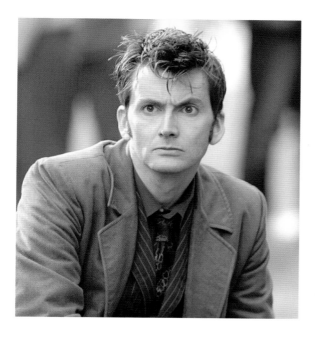

DOCTOR WHO

Voted 'Coolest Man on TV' by the *Radio Times*, David Tennant played out his third series as The Doctor (the tenth), ably accompanied by newcomer Freema Agyeman as his companion Martha Jones, a role played by over 35 actors and actresses. The fourth series began filming over the summer; star guests include Felicity Kendall and Catherine Tate, with Kylie Minogue in the Christmas Special.

The longest-running science fiction series in the world, first aired in November 1963.

In 1969 16.1 million viewers tuned in to watch an episode starring John Cleese.

Peak audience of 7.54 million for 2007 series.

LIFE ON MARS

The second series of *Life on Mars* left viewers hungry for more when it ended on 10 April. The time-travel/cop hybrid garnered a cult following over the 16-episode run. Iconic and subtle references to the 1970s were cleverly interwoven – music of the day, outdated policing practices, archaic technology, lack of political correctness, sexism in the workplace, and the Ford Cortina.

Peak audience of 7.7 million reached for final episode.

The series was named after David Bowie's song 'Life on Mars?'

Channel 4 rejected the original proposal, named Ford Granada, saying: "it's just going to be sillly".

MICHAEL PARKINSON
Talk Show King

26 June: The undisputed star of the British television chat show, known universally as 'Parky', announced that the summer/autumn 2007 series would be his last. He has hosted his own chat show since 1971.

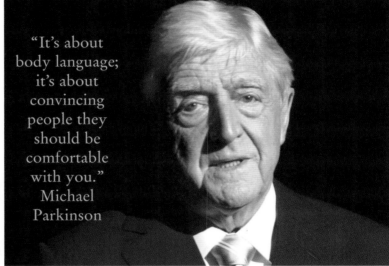

"It's about body language; it's about convincing people they should be comfortable with you."
Michael Parkinson

A proud Yorkshireman, Parky was born in Cudworth, near Barnsley in 1935. After a career as a newspaper and television reporter, he launched his first chat show, in 1971, for the BBC, and it was in this television format that Parkinson excelled. He was relaxed and charming, with a dry Yorkshire wit that put his interviewees at ease, ensuring that he extracted many revelations and extraordinary antics from his subjects. The initial show had an 11 series run (on both BBC1 and BBC2).

Famed guests included Muhammad Ali, Orson Welles, David Niven, Jack Lemmon, Gene Kelly, James Cagney, Kenneth Williams, and a particularly bruising encounter with Rod Hull when Emu attacked him in 1976. After a disagreement with the BBC over the format of the show, he quit in 1982.

In 1998 he made a comeback to the chat show format with *Parkinson*. His guests reflected the new generation of celebrities: Robbie Williams, Geri Halliwell, Ewan McGregor and George Michael amongst others. The series lasted until 2004 when he left the BBC because of a row over his primetime 10 p.m. slot. The show and presenter were quickly snapped up by ITV and ran from 2004–07.

VERA DUCKWORTH
Coronation Street Queen

1 July: It was announced that Vera Duckworth would be leaving *Coronation Street* by the end of the year. The born troublemaker, famous for her indiscretion and played by actress Liz Dawn, first appeared on the show on 19 August 1974.

"It's been an amazing 34 years. I'd like to thank everyone for what has been the best time of my life."
Liz Dawn, aka Vera Duckworth

Vera first entered the series as one of the workers in Mike Baldwin's factory. When she and her husband, Jack, moved into number 9 in 1983, the street would never be the same again. They were the classic comic couple: Jack the hen-pecked husband, Vera the domestic tyrant with the foghorn voice.

Jack's roving eye proved almost too much for Vera at times, but she also had her fair share of indiscretions: most spectacularly in 2000, when she believed that she was about to die during an operation and confessed that Jack wasn't actually the father of her son, Terry, but the product of an earlier fling.

Vera's dreams came true when her name appeared above the door of the legendary Rovers Return. Jack had inherited £30,000 from his brother and the Duckworths bought the pub and became licensees. For the first time the quarrelsome pair became respected members of the community. After predictable financial difficulties they were eventually bought out of the business. Vera and Jack mellowed over the years, but the bickering never stopped.

At the time of writing her route of exit was unknown publicly. But this is not the last we will see of Vera: Liz Dawn, who is 68 years old and suffering from ill health, has agreed to make guest appearances on the show alongside husband Jack, played by Bill Tarmey.

SOAP STARS

BRITISH SOAP AWARDS

CORONATION STREET

Best Soap

Best Actress: Kate Ford (Tracy Barlow)

Best Actor: Antony Cotton (Sean Tully)

Sexiest Male: Rob James-Collier (Liam Connor)

Best Newcomer: Kym Ryder (Michelle Connor)

Best Exit: Bill Ward (Charlie Stubbs)

Best Storyline: Tracy taking revenge on Charlie

EASTENDERS

Best Dramatic Performance: Lacey Turner (Stacey Slater)

EMMERDALE

Best Dramatic Performance from a Young Actor
or Actress: Eden Taylor-Draper (Belle Dingle)

Spectacular Scene of the Year: the house collapse

HOLLYOAKS

Sexiest Female: Roxanne McKee (Louise Summers)

Villain of the Year: Gemma Bissix (Clare Cunningham)

Best Comedy Performance: Gemma Merna (Carmel McQueen)

DOCTORS

Best On-Screen Partnership: Stirling Gallacher
and Sean Gleeson (George and Ronnie Woodson)

Best Single Episode: 'Shreds and Aftermath'

LIFETIME ACHIEVEMENT AWARD

Wendy Richard

Kate Ford, aka Tracy Barlow

Roxanne McKee, aka Louise Summers

Kym Ryder, aka Michelle Connor

Wendy Richard, aka Pauline Fowler

26 May: *Coronation Street* cleaned up at the British Soap Awards, hosted by Philip Schofield and Fern Britten. Surprisingly, *EastEnders* received only one award.

24 September: *Coronation Street* and *EastEnders* won five gongs each at the Inside Soap Awards – it was the first time Corrie has won the Best Soap award in ten years.

INSIDE SOAP AWARDS

Cast of Coronation Street

Lacey Turner and Charlie Clements

Eden Taylor-Draper

CORONATION STREET

Best Soap

Best Actor: Antony Cotton (Sean Tully)

Sexiest Male: Rob James-Collier (Liam Connor)

Best Newcomer: Rob James-Collier (Liam Connor)

Best Bad Boy: Jack P Shepherd (David Platt)

EASTENDERS

Best Actress: Lacey Turner (Stacey Slater)

Best Bitch: Sophie Thompson (Stella Crawford)

Best Couple: Lacey Turner and Charlie Clements
(Stacey and Bradley)

Best-Dressed: Kara Tointon (Dawn Swann)

Best Storyline: Stella's torment of Ben

EMMERDALE

Best Young Actor: Eden Taylor-Draper (Belle Dingle)

Funniest Character: Charlie Hardwick (Val Lambert)

HOLLYOAKS

Sexiest Female: Roxanne McKee (Louise Summers)

THE BILL

Best Drama

"I've won the big one this year, and I'm very, very pleased that they chose me... I don't act because of it but it's nice that someone thinks I'm doing well."
Best Actor Antony Cotton

HAPPY BIRTHDAY BBC RADIO!

Photo taken on 25 July 1968: BBC Radio 1 and Radio 2 DJs celebrated Radio 1's first birthday at Broadcasting House
(top row, left–right) John Peel, David Symonds, Dave Cash, Stuart Henry, Jonny Moran, Alan Freeman; (middle row) Peter Myers, Mike Raven, Terry Wogan, Keith Skues, Kenny Everett, Ed Stewart; (front row) Barry Alldis, Chris Denning, Robin Scott, Tony Blackburn, Sam Costa.

On 30 September BBC Radio 1, 2, 3 and 4 celebrated their 40th anniversary with a number of special programmes and guest appearances by former presenters. On 30 September 1967 the BBC relaunched its national radio services. Radio 1 was a new station designed for younger listeners who had been tuning into the offshore stations; most of these had been closed down in August 1967. Radio 2, 3 and 4 were the new names for the Light Programme, Third Programme and Home Service.

Chris Moyles and Tony Blackburn

"Forty years ago I drove to the studio in an E-type Jaguar, today I drove here in a Smart car. Where have I gone wrong?" Tony Blackburn

Terry Wogan

SPECIAL SHOWS: HIGHLIGHTS

Tony Blackburn, who launched Radio 1 in 1967, joined Chris Moyles to co-host the Breakfast Show.

Annie Nightingale presented a one-off airing of Radio 1's Sunday Night Request Show which she fronted 1982–94.

On Radio 1 there was a 2-hour tribute to John Peel, the veteran broadcaster who died three years ago, entitled 'Keeping it Peel'.

Radio 2 DJ Paul Hollingdale, who opened the network with a breakfast special, returned to talk about his first show.

Spoof DJs Smashie and Nicey were revived by Paul Whitehouse and Harry Enfield, and hosted Pick of the Pops.

Ed Stewart returned with Junior Choice.

Kenny Everett's first Radio 2 broadcast, from 26 years ago, was repeated.

Eddie Mair presented 4 at Forty, a retrospective on Radio 4.

Stephen Fry and Matt Lucas presented a spoof of This is Your Life with Radio 4 as the subject, with contributions from John Humphrys, Sue Lawley, Jonathan Dimbleby and Barry Cryer.

"Radio 1 is still seen as the best radio station in the world… It's a brand that isn't going to go away – it's got a great future."
Bruno Brookes, former disc jockey

MOVIE BRITAIN

It has been a bumper year for British cinemas. UK consumers made 76.9 million visits to the cinema in the first six months of 2007, an increase of 6 per cent on cinema-going in the first half of 2006. As well as some outstanding British films, including the Oscar-winning *The Last King of Scotland*, fans flocked to see blockbuster sequels: *Shrek 3*, *Ocean's Thirteen*, *Pirates of the Caribbean: Dead Man's Chest* and *Spider Man 3*.

The wettest summer since records began contributed to a huge upsurge in viewing figures. Between June and August more than 50 million visits were made to cinemas – a 27 per cent increase on 2006. *The Simpsons Movie* and *Harry Potter and the Order of the Phoenix* were the two biggest summer blockbusters. *The Bourne Ultimatum* also proved very popular. On 20 September *Atonement* was released to great acclaim, earning £6,732,204 in its first three weeks.

The US/UK co-production *Harry Potter and the Order of the Phoenix* achieved record-breaking success; after 10 weeks in the UK box office top 15 it had grossed £49,136,969.

HOT FUZZ The surprise homegrown hit of the year, this police comedy film stars Simon Pegg and Nick Frost. An over-achieving police officer is posted to a sleepy and apparently crime-free village. But this is set to change when a series of murders, disguised as road accidents, shake the village…

Released 14 April. Remained in the UK box office top 15 for eight weeks, during which period it grossed £20,792,585.

NOTES ON A SCANDAL Based on a novel by Zoë Heller and starring Judi Dench and Cate Blanchett, this film charts the intense relationship between a middle-aged single teacher, Barbara, and her young, glamorous colleague, Sheba, who has an affair with a 15-year-old pupil.

Released 2 February. Nominated for the Academy Awards. Remained in the UK box office top 15 for six weeks, during which period it grossed £5,325,389.

MR BEAN'S HOLIDAY Rowan Atkinson proved his credentials as a physical comedian, starring as the well-loved Mr Bean who wins an all-expenses-paid holiday to the Cote d'Azur in a church lottery. All kinds of misadventures and mayhem ensue.

Released 30 March, the film stayed at Number 1 in the UK box office for two weeks, during which period it grossed £13,398,272. In total, it stayed in the box office top 15 for an impressive ten weeks, grossing a total of £22,052,368.

Profile: Helen Mirren

The multiple-award winning actress has taken Hollywood by storm and won fame for her portrayal of two Queen Elizabeths.

Helen Mirren (real name Ilyena Miranov) is the granddaughter of a Tsarist colonel, who came to Britain in 1917. Her father (Vasily Miranov), a taxi-driver and former professional viola player, changed his name to Basil Mirren in the 1950s.

She was born in 1946, in Essex. She auditioned for the National Youth Theatre aged 18, was a star at The Old Vic two years later, and joined the RSC in the late 1960s. Her extensive theatre, TV and film work (previous Oscar nominations for *The Madness of King George* and *Gosford Park*, various Emmys/Baftas and Golden Globes,

especially as DI Jane Tennison in the *Prime Suspect* series and as Elizabeth I in the 2005 Channel 4 series) has regularly led to rave reviews both for her acting and her looks.

She works extensively in support of Oxfam, and speaks passionately on green issues. Despite her republican leanings, she was disappointed not to be able to accept a private invitation to dine with The Queen at Buckingham Palace in May 2007 – "I am not a monarchist. I loathe the British class system… But I grew to fall in love with the Queen. I am a Queenist."

2007: ANNUS MIRABILIS

Best Actress Awards as The Queen: Oscar, Bafta, Golden Globe, Venice Film Festival, Screen Actors Guild, Broadcast Film Critics, National Board of Review, Satellite Awards.

April: Award for 'Distinguished Service to the Arts' from the Critics' Circle.

September: Publication of her autobiography, *In the Frame: My Life in Words and Pictures.*

September: Emmy Television award as Best Actress in a Mini-Series for her performance as Detective Superintendent Jane Tennison in *Prime Suspect: The Final Act.*

"Elizabeth Windsor at the age of 25 walked into literally the role of a lifetime. I honestly feel this award belongs to her, because I think you fell in love with her, not with me."

Helen Mirren

BAFTAS

The Academy Fellowship: Anne V Coates

The Michael Balcon Award For Outstanding British Contribution to Cinema: Nick Daubeny

Film: *The Queen*

The Alexander Korda Award for the Outstanding British Film of the Year: *The Last King of Scotland*

The Carl Foreman Award for Special Achievement by a British Director, Writer or Producer in their First Feature Film: Andrea Arnold (director, *Red Road*)

The David Lean Award for Achievement in Direction: Paul Greengrass (*United 93*)

Original Screenplay: *Little Miss Sunshine*

Adapted Screenplay: *The Last King of Scotland*

Animated Feature Film: *Happy Feet*

Actor in a Leading Role: Forest Whitaker (*The Last King of Scotland*)

Actress in a Leading Role: Helen Mirren (*The Queen*)

Actor in a Supporting Role: Alan Arkin (*Little Miss Sunshine*)

Actress in a Supporting Role: Jennifer Hudson (*Dreamgirls*)

The Orange Rising Star Award: Eva Green

Sunday 11 February:
The 2007 Orange British Academy Film Awards
at the Royal Opera House, Covent Garden, London

HITTING THE

"he was well ablaze, clothing, hair, skin..."

"of course I won't write anything as popular as this again"

HEADLINES

"we were just completely shocked and devastated"

"when these issues happen... we are strong"

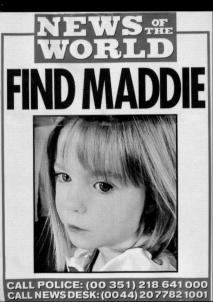

NEWS OF THE **WORLD**

FIND MADDIE

CALL POLICE: (00 351) 218 641 000
CALL NEWS DESK: (0044) 20 7782 1001

PLEASE HELP FIND OUR
MADELEINE

SHE COULD BE NEXT
PLEASE LOOK
IF YOU HAVE ANY INFORMATION

The energy behind The FA Cup

Look into my eyes!
Madeleine McCann was abducted
from Praia Da Luz, Portugal on
03/05/2007

Please could you show
support for her mother
Kate and take the time
to wear a yellow ribbon

Thank you

BRING MADDIE HOME
FROM THE UK
PLEASE RING
0800
555 111
www.findmadeleine.com
FROM ABROAD
PLEASE RING
0044
18 83
73 13 36

NOT AGAIN...

4 August: The first case of Foot and Mouth since 2001 was confirmed at a farm near Guildford, Surrey. It was claimed that the disease spread from a leak at a nearby government laboratory complex.

23 September: Bluetongue – spread by midges from Northern Europe – was confirmed at a rare breeds farm in Suffolk. It was the first ever case in the UK of the disease; an 'outbreak' was declared a few days later.

FOOT & MOUTH DISEASE
Keep Out

"We were just completely shocked and devastated. It felt as if our whole world had been turned upside down."

Surrey farmer Roger Pride, whose cattle were slaughtered after contracting foot and mouth

"We are an economy that has taken the necessary decisions to keep it stable… The decisions we have taken mean the deposits of Northern Rock savers are safe. We have shown that when these issues happen in Britain, we are strong enough to deal with them." Prime Minister Gordon Brown

ROCK SOLID?

14 September: Panicked crowds descended on branches of Northern Rock, reportedly withdrawing a total of £1 billion, after Britain's fifth largest mortgage lender was forced to ask the Bank of England for an emergency line of credit following a 'severe liquidity squeeze' on global markets.

Northern Rock was the first British victim of the 'subprime' crisis in the USA. It was unable to borrow money from international banks, who were cautious about lending money after losing billions of pounds in loans to US mortgage defaulters.

Despite its assets of £113 billion, Newcastle-based Northern Rock could not access ready money to pay off existing debts and give out mortgages.

> "The way the Chancellor and the whole government have handled the Northern Rock incident has been characterised by indecision and confusion."
> George Osborne, Shadow Chancellor

The company had earlier issued a profit warning, and shares in the building society slumped 31 per cent in a single day. Across the country huge queues gathered outside local branches as investors waited patiently to withdraw their savings.

Amid fears that other major banks might be affected, the Treasury took the unprecedented step, on 17 September, of promising to cover all of Northern Rock's deposits, amounting to more than £21 billion.

Shares in Northern Rock recovered slightly and shares in other banks, which had been hit by investors' waning confidence, began to rally. On 25 September Northern Rock announced that it would not be paying an interim share dividend, due on 26 October.

AUTUMN OF DISCONTENT

October: Royal Mail postal workers
embarked on the longest strike at
the Royal Mail for 11 years.

"I want these people back to work." Gordon Brown

"It is hugely disappointing to watch a great British institution
tear itself apart." Millie Banerjee, chair of Postwatch

"Rather than running the business, Royal Mail's actions
demonstrate they are intent on destroying it."
Dave Ward, Communication Workers Union

"It is increasingly evident that the union leadership
are completely out of touch with UK industry and the
reality of how competitive markets work." Royal Mail

Important Notice

Please do not post in this box.
We cannot guarantee a collection from
4th October to 9th October inclusive

Please take your mail to the nearest
Post Office

You can keep up to date with how our services
are affected by going to www.royalmail.com/updates
or by calling 08457 740 740

Royal Mail

A later collection is ma

"He was well ablaze, clothing, hair, skin, and from the attitude he was in, lying on his back, there was a kind of resignation about him, as if he had resigned himself to death."

PC Stewart Ferguson, the off-duty police officer who tackled the suicide bombers

TERROR ALERT

London's West End and Glasgow Airport were targets for car bomb attacks, planned and executed by a group of doctors of foreign descent who all worked in the National Health Service. Neither attack was successful, and there was no loss of life. Eight men were arrested in the aftermath.

On **29 June** two car bombs were discovered in London's West End. The first device, left outside Tiger Tiger nightclub in Haymarket, was reported to police by an ambulance crew who were attending an unrelated incident at the club and noticed fumes.

The car containing the second device, left in Cockspur Street, was illegally parked, and was towed to a pound in Park Lane. Staff noticed a strong smell of petrol and called the police. Forensic examination of the cars revealed that they contained petrol cans, gas canisters and nails, with a mobile phone-based trigger.

On **30 June**, at 3.11 p.m., two men drove a Jeep Cherokee, rigged as a car bomb, into the glass doors of the terminal building at Glasgow Airport. The occupants of the car were apprehended at the scene by two police officers, assisted by members of the general public.

One was badly burnt, and was taken to the Royal Alexandra Hospital, Paisley, where he subsequently died. A suicide note indicated that both men had intended to die in the attack.

The police arrested eight people who were involved in the attacks, all members of the medical profession. Police identified the two Glasgow bombers as Bilal Abdullah, a British-born doctor of Iraqi descent, and Kafeel (also known as Khalid) Ahmed, a doctor of Indian descent.

Police remove the vehicle at Glasgow Airport

"If this was Chelsea or Fulham, this would have been plastered over the front pages."

Carl Minns, Hull Council leader

IT RAINED...

Torrential rainfall in June caused a swathe of floods across the Midlands and northern England. Some of the worst flooding damage was suffered in Hull and its outlying districts. As local authorities struggled to cope with the crisis, many people felt that they had been forgotten by central government.

More than 10,500 homes were evacuated after Hull received a sixth of its annual rainfall in just twelve hours on 25 June. The city's drainage system was overwhelmed and streets and homes began to disappear beneath the rising torrent. An Environment Agency spokesman, Rob Walsh, confirmed that the flooding in Hull was mainly a result of surface water unable to escape: "It would be difficult for any system to deal with that," he said.

Hull residents' calls for help went unanswered for some time. Slow recovery work and a lack of funds targeted at the operation led to Hull being dubbed 'the lost city'.

The different agencies foundered in the aftermath of the floods, and cooperation between agencies was minimal. Hull City Council declared that the city was the victim of a 'humanitarian disaster'. The Council was forced to divert £18 million from a home improvement programme towards the clean-up operation, and a Flood Hardship Fund was launched.

The government awarded Hull £2.15 million in emergency aid, but officials said far more was needed; Residents without insurance were in a desperate predicament, forced to stay with friends or relatives. Many residents may not be able to return to their homes until well into 2008.

Hull Council had no flood insurance, and local taxpayers face a huge bill to repair council properties throughout the city; 3,500 council homes in Hull suffered water damage, together with a dozen schools. Campaigners called the decision not to insure 'folly', since Hull is sited on a known flood plain.

The Council denied rumours that parking tickets were issued to vehicles abandoned in the floods. It said all tickets were suspended between 25 and 29 June.

A 28-year-old man died when his foot became stuck in a flooded drain. His father criticised the attempts of the emergency services to rescue his son. He died from hypothermia after a four-hour rescue operation.

...AND RAINED
20 JULY: THE ISLE OF TEWKESBURY

ELECTION FEVER

Mr Cameron delivered his 8,000-word address without notes, a tour de force which ended a successful Tory conference on a high, confident note. There were accusations that Gordon Brown was running scared, aware that Cameron's conference performance had undermined Labour's lead, and wary of confronting the electorate.

"He's been trying to spin his way into a general election campaign and now he's had to make a humiliating retreat."
David Cameron

6 October: After several weeks of speculation, Gordon Brown announced that he would not be going to the polls in November.

Confronted by the Tories' surprise announcement at their Party Conference that they were planning to raise the inheritance tax threshold to £1 million, Brown's advisers feared that Labour's majority would be challenged at the polls, especially in the marginal seats.

"I'll not be calling an election. I have a vision for change in Britain and I want to show people how in government we're implementing it." Gordon Brown

HOSTAGE

4 April: Fifteen Royal Navy personnel, captured by Iranian Revolutionary Guards who claimed they were in national waters, were released after 12 days in captivity.

> "I was frozen in terror and just stared into the darkness of my blindfold... I wasn't going to let them see me cry."
>
> Arthur Batchelor

The Government disputed Iranian allegations, and intense diplomatic efforts were made to secure the captives' release. A videotape, broadcast on 28 March, showed the detainees, including the only woman, Faye Turner, who apologised for their intrusion into Iranian waters. On 4 April President Ahmadinejad proclaimed that the captives would be released as an Easter 'gift' to Britain. On 8 April the MoD announced they would be allowed to publish their stories. This decision provoked public outrage and permission was subsequently withdrawn.

FREEDOM

4 July: The BBC correspondent kidnapped in Gaza by the militant group Army of Islam was released after 114 days in captivity and a worldwide campaign for his freedom.

> "It was like being buried alive."

Alan Johnston

DIARY OF CAPTIVITY

12 March: Alan Johnston's car is found abandoned in Gaza City on 12 March. The BBC confirms that it is "concerned for his safety".

26 March: Rallies and vigils, held at the BBC on Mondays, become a weekly event.

9 May: A videotape from a group calling itself Jaish al-Islam (Army of Islam) is released. It shows a picture of Johnston's BBC identity card, but no pictures of him. The UN envoy appeals for his release.

16 May: Special celebrations are held to mark Johnston's 45th birthday.

1 June: A video is released on the internet showing the first pictures of Alan Johnston since his abduction.

20 June: Thousands of colleagues around the world hold a vigil to mark Johnston's 100th day in captivity.

24 June: A new video of Johnston is released, wearing what he says is an explosives vest, which will be detonated if force is used to free him.

2 July: Hamas security forces in Gaza seize several members of the Army of Islam.

4 July: Alan Johnston is freed and handed to Hamas.

SO NEAR...

Lewis Hamilton's sensational rookie year ended in disappointment as he was pipped to the F1 title by Kimi Raikkonen at the Brazilian Grand Prix on 21 October.

"Who'd have thought I'd be ranked number two in my first year of Formula One? It's been a crazy year and I honestly can't say I'm really gutted – I'm not. I finished second in the World Championship. I beat my team mate under extremely difficult circumstances. I beat the two-time world champion. That was the goal. Who would have thought I would be leading the World Championship going into the last race?"

Lewis Hamilton

"South Africa deserve to win... But it's disappointing. We gave it everything. At times we got close enough and we never really felt we were going to lose. We had a lot of ground to catch up in this tournament and the guys all took the responsibility... It has been a hell of a journey."
Jonny Wilkinson, 20 October

BIG WINNERS

11 October: A consortium led by Royal Bank of Scotland started to take control of Dutch bank ABN AMRO after the success of its record-breaking bid of 70 billion euros (£49bn), the world's largest ever hostile bank takeover, was confirmed.

The RBS-led consortium formally declared victory after shareholders representing 86 per cent of the Dutch bank's shares accepted their offer. Arthur Martinez, chairman of ABN's supervisory board, said the consortium's offer was an "absolute victory" for the bank's shareholders. Previously, Barclays had admitted defeat for its bid, after a six-month battle.

RBS chief executive Fred Goodwin and his counterparts at Santander of Spain and Fortis, the Belgo-Dutch group, will join ABN's supervisory board in the move.

This record-breaking deal is the largest ever hostile cross-border takeover of a substantial banking group. It is also the most complex large scale corporate break-up to be attempted in the sector.

On 12 October the victorious consortium consolidated its hold over ABN Amro by nominating Mark Fisher, a RBS executive, to head the Dutch bank. ABN's Management Board Chairman, Rijkman Groenink, who was in favour of the rival bid from Barclays, stepped down with a reported pay-off of £20 million following 33 years' service.

"There won't be a bubbly moment, I've got a funny feeling we will be getting straight into the hard work moment."
Sir Fred Goodwin, chief executive, RBS Group

10 August: Angela Kelly, a postal worker from East Kilbride, landed an enormous £35.425 million in the EuroMillions lottery, the largest lottery win ever in the UK.

Ms Kelly, who earns £21,000 a year, is separated from her husband and lives with her 14-year-old son. She only discovered her win three days after the draw, when she checked the lucky dip ticket in her handbag.

Her jackpot win is £17 million higher than the previous British EuroMillions record.

> "I couldn't even say anything, I just pushed my chair back and put my head between my knees."
>
> Angela Kelly

The record-breaking train left Paris at 10.44 (local time) and was driven by French driver, Francis Queret, who handed over the controls to his English counterpart, Neil Meare, half-way through the Channel. The train arrived at St Pancras at just before 11.48 (UK time), a total journey time of 2 hours, 3 minutes, 39 seconds. For scheduled services, the new line is expected to shave 20 minutes off journey times, cutting it to 2 hours 15 minutes. Built at a cost of £73.5 million per mile, the new railway line, known as High Speed 1, runs for 68 miles from Folkestone, Kent, through the £100-million Ebbsfleet International station near Dartford, to the new international terminal at a refurbished St Pancras.

> "Today marks Britain's entry into the European high-speed rail club."
> Richard Brown, chief executive, Eurostar

FAST FACTS

Journey time: 2 hours, 3 mins, 39 secs

Cost: The new railway line and revamp of St Pancras cost £5.8 billion

Top speed reached: 200 mph

Tunnels: A quarter of the new 68-mile-long route consists of tunnels

Bridges: There are 152 bridges along the new route

Man hours: Over 53 million worked during the construction

Excavations: Over 16.5 million cubic metres of earth were removed

Projected passengers per year: 10 million on Eurostar by 2010

2:3:39

4 September: Eurostar set a new record on its inaugural journey on a new high-speed line, the first to be built in Britain for 100 years.

GRAND
St Pancras: London's Pride

A total of £800 million has been spent redeveloping St Pancras station, a London icon, which opened to Eurostar passengers on 14 November. The original station, designed by Gilbert Scott, was opened in 1868, and became famous for its neo-Gothic façade and majestic single span roof. But over the course of the 20th century it fell into disrepair and was even threatened with demolition. The central focus of the station is The Meeting Place, a £1 million, 9-metre-high bronze sculpture by British artist Paul Day, showing a young couple embracing. It was unveiled on 14 February 2007.

FACT FILE

Total cost of reconstruction: £800 million

234-foot roof has been re-glazed, using 18,000 panes of glass

Reconstruction has utilised 60 million bricks and 300,000 Welsh slate tiles

82,000 square feet of retail space is available

The station boasts Europe's longest champagne bar, at over 90 metres

OPENINGS

O₂: A Breathtaking Venue

The ill-fated Millennium Dome was seen by many as a white elephant. But it underwent a renaissance in 2007 when, after a £500 million redevelopment, it reopened in June as the O₂ Arena, a vast concert venue, music club, cinema and exhibition space.

FACT FILE

Venue seats 20,000 – its volume is equal to thirteen Albert Halls, ten St Paul's Cathedrals or two old Wembley Stadiums

It has a one-kilometre circumference and is 50 metres high at its central point. The steel masts protruding from the dome are each 100 metres high

The Dome will be part of a massive £5 billion regeneration of the surrounding Greenwich Peninsula

Bon Jovi were the first act to play there on 24 June

Prince began a mammoth 21-night concert series on 2 August, setting a new record for the most nights in one arena

The Rolling Stones played for three nights in August. Wood and Richards flouted the smoking ban on stage

Tutankhamun and The Golden Age of the Pharoahs opened on 15 November in the O₂ bubble exhibition space. This was the exhibition that attracted over 1.8 million people in 1972

About 20 million fans rushed to register for tickets for Led Zeppelin's reunion gig in November. Tickets were allocated via a ballot – 80,000 fans per minute attempted to register online

"Of course I won't write anything as popular as this again, but I have truthfully known that since 1999, when the thing began to become a little bit insane. So I've had a good long time to know that, and I accept it." J K Rowling

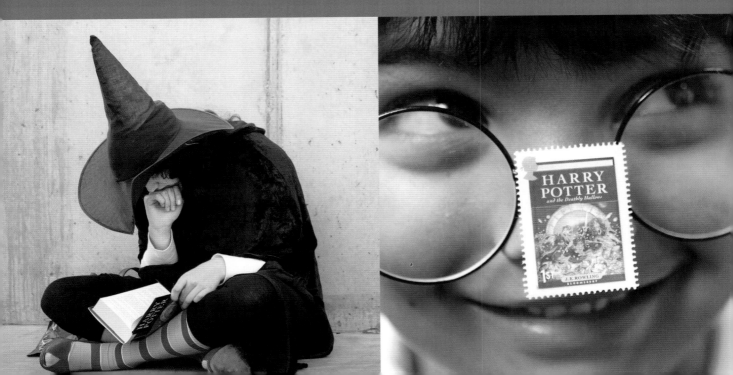

POTTERMANIA

00:01a.m., Saturday 21 July: the final Harry Potter is published

HP7 FACTS

Harry Potter and the Deathly Hallows is the fastest selling book in UK history.

In the UK, more than one household in ten bought a copy in the first 24 hours.

More than two million copies were sold in advance on Amazon alone.

It was published simultaneously in English in more than 90 countries worldwide.

ChildLine organised for extra staff to be on duty, anticipating that readers might need support if any of their best-loved characters were killed off.

Devotees came from all over Europe and the USA for the UK launch. Fans camped outside bookshops for three nights.

Approximately 325 million Harry Potter books have been sold in 64 different languages in the last decade.

Author J K Rowling launched the new book with a live reading session at the Natural History Museum in London. She signed 250 copies an hour.

J K Rowling is one of the richest women in the UK, worth around £545 million.

£50m

3 June–7 July: Damien Hirst's masterpiece, For the Love of God, is made of platinum, diamonds and human teeth and was exhibited in the Beyond Belief exhibition at the White Cube gallery. The skull is encrusted with 8,601 diamonds.

30 August: The skull was reportedly bought by an unnamed group of investors for £50 million cash. The investors include Hirst, so that he can retain some control over the skull's future.

"It works much better than I imagined. I was slightly worried that we'd end up with an Ali G ring."

Damien Hirst

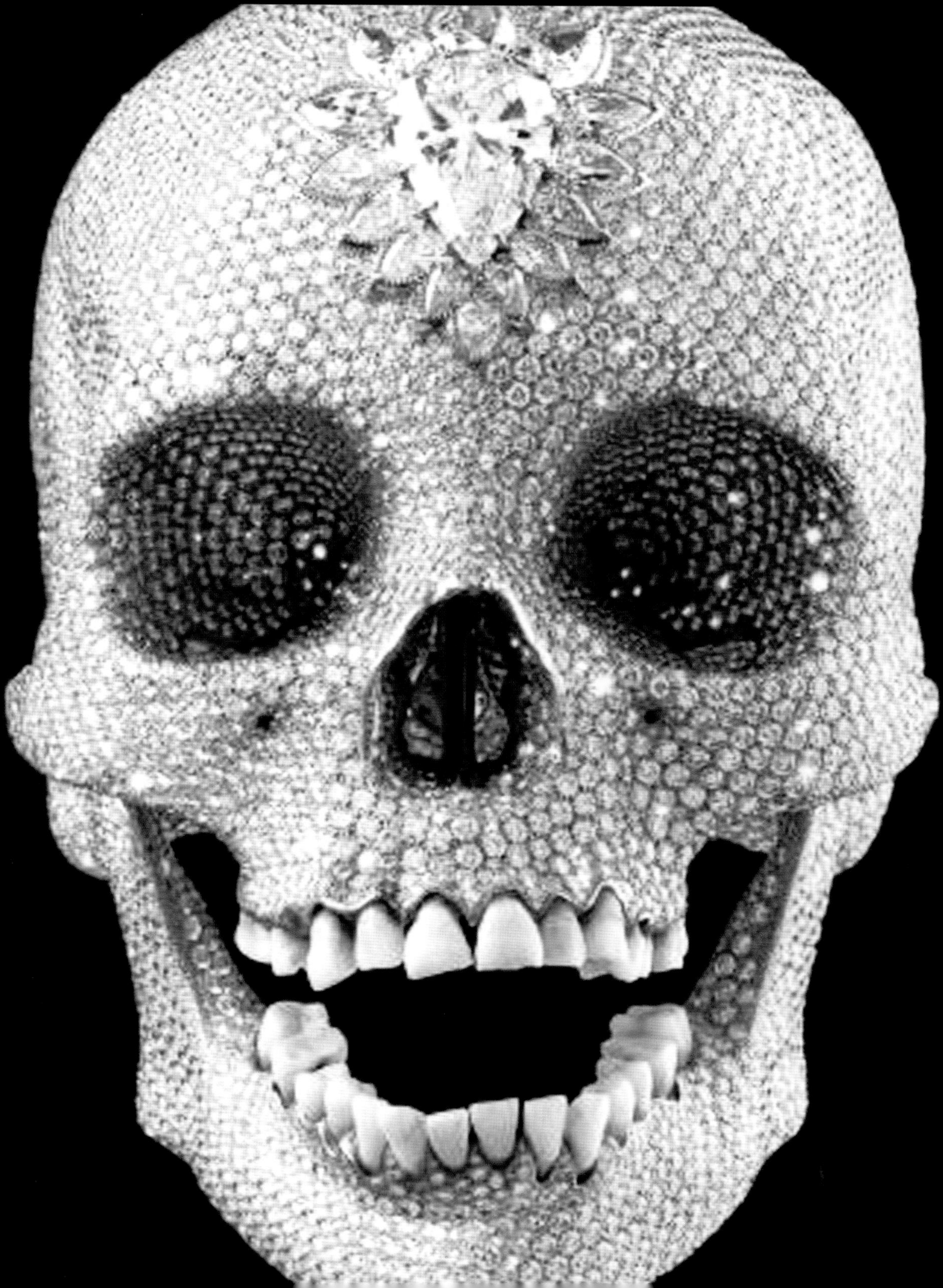

HAPPY

20 years since Kylie's first single came out in Oz
20th anniversary of the Big Storm that devastated parts of southern England
Silver jubilee (25 years) of Channel 4
30 years since Elvis died
30th anniversary of *Star Wars*
40th anniversary of the death of guerrilla Che Guevara in Bolivia
40th anniversary of Radio 1, 2, 3 & 4
40th anniversary of *Sergeant Pepper's Lonely Hearts Club Band*
40 years since first cashpoint machine appeared
40 years since *Rolling Stone* magazine was launched
40th anniversary of first breathalyser test, known as the drunkometer
50th anniversary of the Treaty of Rome, which created the Common Market
50 years since the first broadcast of *The Sky at Night*, presented by Patrick Moore
50th anniversary of Russian launch of first satellite, Sputnik
Golden Jubilee (50 years) of Liverpool's Cavern Club
50th anniversary of first Premium Bond draw – the top prize was £1,000
50th anniversary of Britain's first television soap, *Emergency Ward 10*
50th anniversary of the Frisbee (or 'toy flying saucer')

BIRTHDAY!

Diamond (60th) wedding anniversary of The Queen and Prince Philip
Christian Dior 60th anniversary
Pucci 60th anniversary
60th anniversary of photo-finish cameras, first used at Epsom
75th anniversary of telephone directory enquiries
75th anniversary of book tokens, first issued by the Booksellers Association
75th anniversary of the first royal Christmas broadcast
80th anniversary of National Car Parks
80th anniversary of first transatlantic phone call, from New York to London
Caravan Club celebrates 100 years
100 years since Scouts held first camp
The centenary of London taxis with meters
125 years of the Ashes, the longest continuously running international sporting contest
150th anniversary of the Indian Mutiny
200th anniversary of gas lighting, on Pall Mall, London
300th anniversary of the Act of Union between England and Scotland
400th anniversary of Guy Fawkes night, first celebrated in Bristol
800th anniversary of the cities of Liverpool and Leeds

POLITICS

"we are pleased that the Iraqi army are now taking over"

"I believe Northern Ireland has come to a time of peace"

"I could sense a juggernaut moving my way"

"that's it... the end"

THE BLAIR YEARS

Tony Blair resigned as Prime Minister in June, earlier than he had wanted to leave, but after a longer stretch in Number 10 than the vast majority of its previous occupants.

"That's it. The end," he said at the final curtain, a crack in his voice and appearing close to tears when he delivered his farewell performance in the Commons after more than a decade of domination over British politics. As an election winner, his record was unrivalled in modern times, his hat-trick of successive victories matched only by Margaret Thatcher and his accumulated parliamentary majorities greater even than hers.

Labour, the serial losers of British politics before Blair, were turned into the most successful party of the centre-left in Europe. The Conservatives were consigned to bitter years in the wilderness of opposition. John Major, William Hague, Iain Duncan Smith and Michael Howard could not beat Blair. So the Tories finally resorted to trying to copy him with David Cameron.

Blair was the least Labour of Labour Prime Ministers. Ideologically, he was of no fixed abode. He preferred to define his politics not by reference to Left and Right, but in terms of modernity. A consistent theme of his premiership was a restless desire to change old institutions, whether they were the Labour Party, the National Health Service or the House of Lords. That quest for modernisation could be a weakness when it expressed itself in shallow glamour projects which did not live up to their hype. Blair persisted with the expensive folly of the Millennium Dome against the wishes of the majority of the Cabinet. It was characteristic of his centralised style of governing that he simply ignored the doubts of his senior Ministers.

He had limited personal interest in constitutional reform, but it is one of the paradoxes of his premiership that he left behind large and irreversible changes to the shape of the United Kingdom. The axe was swung on the hereditary peers and most of them were removed from the Lords. Scotland gained a parliament for the first time since the Act of Union. The Welsh got an assembly for the first time ever. After eight years of rule by a Labour-Liberal Democrat coalition, some of Blair's private fears about devolution became a reality shortly before he left office when the Scots elected a minority Nationalist government.

He was a leader with many gifts, not the least of which was being the most accomplished political communicator of his generation. At times of national drama and international crisis, he had a great gift for sensing, articulating and fashioning the public mood. When the Royal Family froze in self-endangering silence after the death of Diana, Blair stepped into the role of spokesman for national emotion with his word wreath to 'the People's Princess'. He made success out of a crisis again in the aftermath of 9/11 when he gave more eloquent expression to the shock and gravity of those atrocities than any other world leader. He spoke more resonantly for America than its own President. When Britain won the bid to stage the Olympics, many neutral observers judged that Blair's personal charm had been vital to securing the Games over France and his old adversary, Jacques Chirac.

> As an election winner, his record was unrivalled in modern times, his hat-trick of successive victories matched only by Margaret Thatcher.

The first baby-boomer to reach Downing Street, and the first of its occupants to have a baby while at Number 10 since the 19th century, he understood the 24/7 media and modern culture in a way that none of his predecessors had. Comfortable on the soft sofas of chatshow television, he was the first celebrity Prime Minister.

Extremely talented at the thespian dimension of politics, he was less accomplished at the practical prose of governing. He was an actor politician not an engineer politician. Margaret Jay, who served in his Cabinet as Leader of the Lords, coined a phrase for the look that would come over the Prime Minister's face when he was presented with policy detail that he found tedious. She called it "the garden look". He would lose focus as his attention drifted away and out of the window overlooking the back garden of Number 10.

This was a significant handicap which was compounded by his absolute lack of experience of government when he arrived at Number 10. A mastery of the machinery was essential for Blair to

> Extremely talented at the thespian dimension of politics, he was less accomplished at the practical prose of governing. He was an actor politician not an engineer politician.

deliver his central promise to provide Britain with world-class public services. A decade of sustained prosperity – his was the first Labour Government not to be shipwrecked by economic crisis – allowed unprecedented sums to be poured into public services. By the end of his decade, spending per pupil in state schools had doubled and the budget of the NHS rose by a similar magnitude. The results of that spending could be seen in new school buildings and hospitals, and the employment of thousands more teachers, nurses and doctors. Exam results improved and waiting times fell. But it was very moot whether all that extra money was effectively spent.

Reform was too slow and too muddled and less radical than Blair had hoped, much to his enduring regret. He took until the end of his first term to work out how he wanted to change schools and the health service. His belief that standards would be driven up by competition and choice put him on a collision course with much of his own party. While he emphasised excellence, they were still attached to equality. Only by a perilously narrow margin did he win the second term vote to boost the funding of universities through the introduction of variable tuition fees. He could only get his third term schools reforms through parliament with the support of the Conservatives.

The gap between public expectations and reality was too often filled by spin. This was the shorthand for the techniques of manipulating the media and public opinion that Labour had practised to such great effect when in opposition. In Government, spin became counter-productive. It encouraged cynicism in the media and mistrust among the public. Blair's ambitions were also frustrated by his perpetual conflicts with Gordon Brown, his Chancellor and heir-all-too-apparent. It was common to describe Blair's style as 'presidential'. In truth, New Labour was more like a dual monarchy. When Blair and Brown were working together, they were pretty much unstoppable. When they were fighting each other, the Government was poisoned into paralysis.

Cherie, his wife, was the most insistent voice urging Blair to strike against his mighty Chancellor and the rival government that he ran from the Treasury. Though Blair fingered the dagger on several occasions, he never felt sufficiently strong or bold to wield the knife. Brown's implacable hostility was not the only reason, but it was a hugely important one, that Blair failed to realise his goal of taking Britain into the European single currency.

Blair was bolder, for good and bad, when he was operating in areas where he was liberated from his Chancellor. This was most true of foreign affairs. The first major foreign crisis of his premiership erupted in the spring of 1999 when Slobodan Milosevic, the dictator of Serbia, began to ramp up the violence

There was a highly damaging caricature of Blair... as a poodle of Bush. The reality was that Blair was a true believer in the project that had been activated by 9/11 to remove Saddam Hussein and reorder the Middle East.

against the Muslim population of Kosovo. Blair's hawkish insistence that the Serbian dictator could not be allowed to prevail was in striking contrast to the equivocations of other European leaders and the vacillations of Bill Clinton, his enfeebled ally in the White House. In the Kosovo crisis, Blair found a role for himself on the world stage that he relished and a moral purpose for his premiership. The defeat of Milosevic was a high point for his belief in liberal interventionism and his conviction that military force could and should be used in the cause of democracy and human rights.

That success sowed the seeds of later disaster. It led him to make the fateful decision to bind himself to George W Bush and join the American President's invasion of Iraq. There was a highly damaging caricature of Blair, as pervasive as it was inaccurate, as a poodle of Bush. The reality was that Blair was a true believer in the project that had been activated by 9/11 to remove Saddam Hussein and reorder the Middle East.

The conventional war which started in early 2003 was over in three weeks and won with deceptive ease. It was the peace that was catastrophically lost. The Americans had no proper post-war plan, with the result that Iraq descended into the hellish combination of sectarian violence and terrorist insurgency. Such was Blair's despair that he came extremely close to resigning in the spring of 2004.

Amplifying this disaster for his reputation was the failure to find any of the weapons of mass destruction that he had presented as the justification for the conflict. This shattered his credibility with much of the public and fractured his relationship with his own party. The greatest personal tragedy for him was that Iraq severely discredited the cause of liberal interventionism for which he had been such a compelling advocate. His credibility problem was exacerbated by the sleaze eruptions which became a regular feature of his premiership after he failed to heed the early warning of the Ecclestone Affair. Several members of his Government were forced to resign from the Cabinet: twice in the cases of Peter Mandelson and David Blunkett.

The most damaging of these episodes was the cash-for-coronet allegations which led Blair to gain the unenviable distinction of being the first British Prime Minister to be interviewed by the police in the course of an investigation into criminal corruption. Though this saga ended without any prosecutions, the long police inquiry was a toxic cloud over the final chapter of Blair's premiership.

This was one of the factors that made him vulnerable to the internal revolt which erupted in the autumn of 2006. Though he had won a third election victory the previous spring, it was with a reduced majority and a very low share of the vote. It was a victory that tasted like defeat. From that moment on, supporters of Gordon Brown ratcheted up the pressure for Blair to surrender the crown to the best friend who had

turned into his deadliest rival. Faced with a mounting clamour for his departure from his own MPs, in September 2006 Blair was compelled to announce that he would leave Number 10 within a year.

His consolation was that he secured the time and space to bring one of his most important projects to a conclusion. Even his most severe critics credit him with a great achievement in Northern Ireland. The Good Friday Agreement hammered out in the Easter of 1998 led on to the declaration from the IRA that their 'war' was over, the most peaceful period in Northern Ireland's history in more than three decades, and a power-sharing government between Unionists and Nationalists in Belfast. The years of tortuous negotiation to cajole the parties towards agreement showed Blair's qualities at their most effective. The reconciliation of previously implacable enemies was testimony to his negotiating skills, his talent for creative ambiguity, his capacity to take risks, his optimism in the face of adversity, and his willingness to expend vast amounts of time, ingenuity and energy in a cause he believed in.

Not everything he did will outlast Tony Blair, but there is no argument that he transformed his country and transfigured its politics. His personal appeal had withered by the time he left office, but his governing idea remained dominant. Both Gordon Brown and David Cameron subscribe to his belief that economic success can be combined with social justice and decent public services. Both Labour and the Tories have converged on his ground.

Many occupants of Number 10 merely preside over their time. Tony Blair has an extremely good claim to belong in that select company of Prime Ministers who define an era.

"I can say to you today that I believe Northern Ireland has come to a time of peace, a time when hate will no longer rule. How good it will be to be part of the wonderful healing in this province today." Ian Paisley

NORTHERN IRELAND: A NEW DAWN

Bitter enemies, who represented the polarised extremes of Northern Ireland's divided past, came together in a new power-sharing government at Stormont, ending years of enmity.

On 8 May, Ian Paisley, the leader of the Democratic Unionist Party, took office as Northern Ireland's first minister, with his former enemy, Martin McGuinness of Sinn Fein, taking over as deputy leader. They appeared relaxed and jovial as they were sworn in – an extraordinary end to the 'Troubles' that had claimed 3,700 lives.

Heading a new 12-member administration, they will take back control of government departments that have been run from London over the past five years.

Ian Paisley had always insisted that the IRA must renounce terrorism before he would consider any kind of alliance with Sinn Fein. When Sinn Fein recognised the legitimacy of the Northern Irish police force the final barrier was removed. The spectre of Britain and Dublin claiming joint sovereignty convinced Paisley that power-sharing with Catholics was a lesser evil.

The union was a crowning achievement for Tony Blair who, with his Irish counterpart, Bertie Ahern, had worked hard to bring the two opposing sides together since 1998.

HISTORY OF THE CONFLICT

1921: Northern Ireland is formed from six provinces, opting out of a self-government agreement.

1967–68: Catholics demonstrate against Unionist power in Northern Ireland.

1972: Direct rule of Northern Ireland from London begins. British troops are targeted; 470 people are killed during the conflict's bloodiest year.

1994: Mostly Catholic Irish Republican Army (IRA) announces a cease-fire. It lasts until February 1996, when the IRA sets off a bomb in London, killing two.

1998: The Good Friday peace accord is endorsed by voters in Ireland and Northern Ireland.

2005: IRA agreement to disarm clears way for implementation of the agreement. Blair and Ahern encourage a move to home rule and shared power.

2007: Voters elect a new assembly on 7 March, giving the Protestant and Catholic political parties the power to form an executive government (deadline 7 May).

FAREWELL TO BASRA?

3 September: British troops completed their withdrawal from central Basra, southern Iraq, paving the way for the withdrawal of the main British force from Iraq in 2008.

The flag of the 4th Battalion The Rifles was lowered inside the compound of Basra Palace, a magnet for daily insurgent attacks, as a bugler sounded the retreat and – with the raising of Iraqi flag – the handover to provincial Iraqi control began.

A total of 550 remaining British soldiers were withdrawn from Basra Palace. They joined the rest of the British military mission, consisting of 5,000 servicemen and women, which is now based at Basra air base, 13 miles from the city, where they remain on standby in case the security situation deteriorates.

British troops had been in the city for four years, following the invasion of Iraq in 2003. While some Iraqis in the streets cheered the British departure, Colonel Bob Stewart, who led British forces in Bosnia, conceded that Basra was still 'lawless' after four years of occupation. Control of the city is now largely in the hands of Iranian-backed Shia militias. But Iraqi government forces insist that they will be able to fill the 'security vacuum' left by the departing British.

The British troop withdrawal took place against a background of criticism from US commentators, who alleged that the British had lost control in Basra. General Sir Mike Jackson, the former head of the British Army, called US strategy in Iraq "intellectually bankrupt".

In 2007 there were 37 British fatalities in Basra between 13 January and 8 August alone. The Prime Minister has refused to set a timetable for the eventual withdrawal of all British forces from Iraq.

"We are pleased that the Iraqi army are now taking over the situation – we as an Iraqi people reject occupation, we reject colonialism – we want our freedom." Rudha Muter, Basra resident

"It's an admission that the sort of role which has been performed from Basra Palace is no longer effective. I see this as a necessary step towards what I believe to be the withdrawal which would be in the interests of British forces." Sir Menzies Campbell, former Liberal Democrat leader

"We are staying to discharge our obligations to the Iraqi people and the international community." Prime Minister Gordon Brown

ABOLITION OF SLAVERY

The 200th anniversary of the Abolition of the Slave Trade Act on 25 March 1707 was remembered

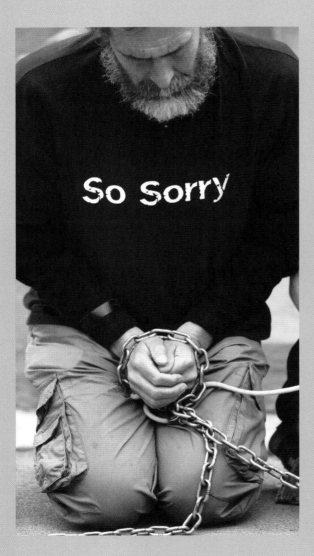

A programme of events – from exhibitions at the British Museum and V&A to the launch of the replica ship 'Amistad' – marked this anniversary year. On 27 March 'Set All Free', a national service of commemoration at Westminster Abbey, was attended by The Queen and Tony Blair. On 23 August, the date marked by the slave rebellion on Haiti in 1791, the International Slavery Museum opened in Liverpool and in London Mayor Ken Livingstone inaugurated the capital's first annual memorial day. He also called for a national day of remembrance.

"I offer an apology on behalf of London and its institutions for their role in the transatlantic slave trade... It was the racial murder of not just those who were transported but generations of enslaved African men, women and children. To justify this murder and torture, black people had to be declared inferior or not human. We live with the consequences today." Ken Livingstone

"I believe the bicentenary offers us a chance not just to say how profoundly shameful the slave trade was... but also to express our deep sorrow that it ever happened..." Tony Blair

THE FALKLANDS

Ceremonies marked the 25th anniversary of the end of the Falklands War on 14 June 1982

A week of commemorations across the country was launched at a memorial service in the Falkland Islands Memorial Chapel, Pangbourne College, Berkshire, attended by The Queen, Tony Blair, and former PM Baroness Thatcher.

It climaxed on 17 June with a service in Horse Guards Parade, London, attended by 10,000 veterans. A flypast by more than 50 aircraft representing squadrons that flew in 1982, including Typhoon fighter jets, Sea King helicopters and the Royal Air Force's Red Arrows, ended the memorial.

The Falklands conflict lasted 74 days. A total of 255 British servicemen were killed, and three islanders lost their lives. More than 650 Argentinians were killed.

> "Aggression was defeated and reversed. The wishes of local people were upheld as paramount. Britain's honour and interests prevailed."
>
> Baroness Thatcher

CASH FOR HONOURS

20 March: Police handed over a 216-page report on the affair, which had reportedly cost over £1 million, to the Crown Prosecution Service. In July the CPS announced that there was insufficient evidence to prosecute.

"I have decided that there is insufficient evidence to provide a realistic prospect of conviction against any individual for any offence in relation to this matter."

Carmen Dowd, CPS, 20 July

In March 2006 allegations that peerages had been 'sold' to four wealthy businessmen who had donated over £14 million to the Labour Party were turned over to the police. All four nominations had subsequently been blocked by the House of Lords Commission.

Investigating officers made a number of high profile arrests, including Lord Levy, Tony Blair's chief fundraiser, and Downing Street aide Ruth Turner. In an unprecedented experience for a serving prime minster, Tony Blair was interviewed three times by the police. Virtually all the cabinet ministers involved in the 2005 election campaign were questioned in writing about fundraising.

The CPS decision drew a line under the affair, though in the words of Menzies Campbell, "This whole affair has diminished politics and politicians in the eyes of the public."

THE CAMPBELL DIARIES

9 July: Alastair Campbell published his diaries, billed as the "inside story of the Blair years". The final work spans 1994–2003, and is 350,000 words in length, edited down from 2.5 million.

1 May 1997, the Labour election victory: "I said to TB, this is so weird, you've worked so hard for so long for something, it comes, you're surrounded by people who are so happy because of what you've achieved, yet you don't feel like they do, and you just want to get home to bed."

31 December 1999, party at the Dome: "The Queen arrived with Philip, Anne and her husband. Apart from the Queen, who at least managed the odd smile, the others looked very pissed off to be there. TB worked away at them, trying to charm them into the mood, but Anne was like granite."

11 September 2001, on hearing of New York attacks: "We got on a train… and I remember thinking, God, this is bloody ridiculous, he's the prime minister and he's shuffling about trying to find a seat."

On negotiations for the Good Friday agreement: "It showed TB at his infuriating best. Once he got the bit between his teeth, and decided to go for it, he always knew best... he was like a man possessed."

"I could sense a juggernaut moving my way."

On hearing of David Kelly's suicide, 18 July 2003

GORDON BROWN

During his ten-year period as Chancellor, Gordon Brown oversaw a period of sustained economic growth. In June he finally succeeded Tony Blair as Prime Minister.

GORDON'S YEAR

January: As speculation about his future continued to rumble, the media reported that Brown had finally "dropped any pretence of not wanting, or expecting, to move into Number 10 in the next few months".

March: Lord Turnbull, who worked as Brown's Permanent Secretary at the Treasury from 1998 until 2002, accused Brown of running the Treasury with "Stalinist ruthlessness" and treating Cabinet colleagues with "more or less complete contempt".

27 June: Brown succeeded Tony Blair as Prime Minister, three days after becoming Leader of the Labour Party.

June: Although still committed to the Iraq War, he said in a speech that he would "learn the lessons" from the mistakes that have been made in Iraq. Some have suggested that Brown has been trying to distance himself from the close relationship that Tony Blair and George Bush enjoyed, but Brown himself has vehemently denied this.

September/October: Brown enjoyed a successful first party conference as PM in Bournemouth. In early October the Tories claimed that his decision not to hold an autumn election was a humiliating retreat.

CAMPAIGNING PROMISES

Brown's leadership campaign promised some policy initiatives, suggesting that a Brown-led government would introduce:

An end to corruption: As a result of the cash for honours scandal, Brown's words have led to a belief that he'll bring in a new ministerial code which sets out clear standards of behaviour for ministers.

Constitutional reform: During his campaign he said he wants a "better constitution" that is "clear about the rights and responsibilities of being a citizen in Britain today". It is not clear whether he proposes a US-style written constitution – something the UK has never had – or a looser bill of rights.

Housing: Housing planning restrictions are likely to be relaxed. Brown has said he wants to release more land and ease access to ownership with shared equity releases. He backed a proposal to build five new eco towns, each housing between 10,000 and 20,000 homeowners – up to 100,000 new houses in total.

Health: Brown intends to have GPs' surgeries open at the weekends. He stated that the NHS was his "top priority", yet as Chancellor he had just cut the annual budget of the English NHS from £6.2bn to £4.2bn.

ESSENTIAL FACTS

Born 20 February 1951

Married to Sarah Macaulay

First child, Jennifer, was born
prematurely and died

Second child, John, born in 2003

Third child, James, born in 2006,
diagnosed with cystic fibrosis

Chancellor of the Exchequer in Tony
Blair's government 1997–2007,
becoming the United Kingdom's
longest serving Chancellor, and
overseeing the longest period of
sustained economic growth in the
history of the UK

"I've got a
programme of
change for the
future. Do I need
to call an election to
do so? No. The right
thing to do is to get
on with the job."
Gordon Brown
in September

15 October: Sir Menzies Campbell stepped down from the leadership of the Liberal Democrats. A decision on the new leader is expected by 17 December. Sir Menzies felt that questions about his leadership were "getting in the way of further progress by the party".

Sir Menzies Campbell had taken over the leadership of the Liberal Democrats from Charles Kennedy in January 2006. An expert on foreign policy, with a formidable intelligence and grasp of complex issues, 'Ming' was seen by many in his party as too old for the job. He had not been able to contend for the leadership when Paddy Ashdown stepped down because he was fighting a battle with cancer, and had to content himself with becoming Charles Kennedy's deputy.

His maturity and gravitas, formerly an asset, did not serve him well in the hurly burly of Prime Minister's Questions, and many thought that he did not compare favourably with the youthful David Cameron. The 'young turks' in the party began to deride his lacklustre leadership.

Speculation grew about the Lib Dem leadership, especially in the wake of Gordon Brown's decision not to call an early general election. An ICM poll on the weekend of 13/14 October suggested that Conservative support was at 43 per cent with Labour on 36 per cent and the Lib Dems on just 14 per cent. Senior party figures felt that they could not allow the perceived hiatus in the leadership to drift on any longer. If a new, dynamic leader was to be elected, the decision had to be made soon in order to maximise the impact on voters before the next election.

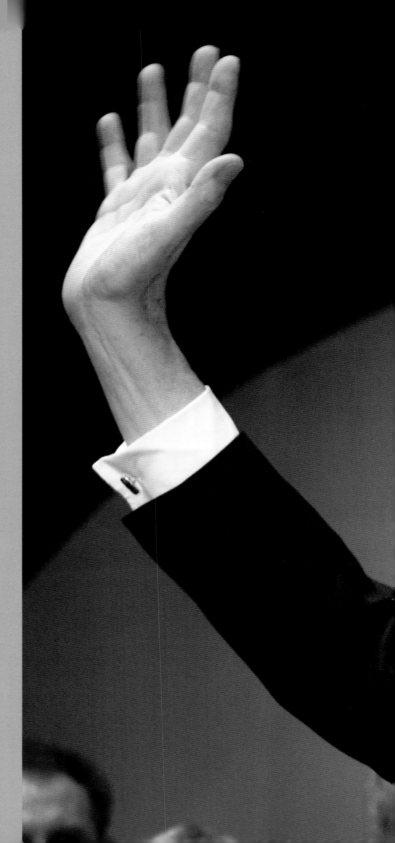

MENZIES
STEPS DOWN

MUSIC AND

"Primark is just as good as Gucci"

"this year has been the year of the celebrity scent"

FASHION

"this has been the most perfect way of remembering her"

"she's reckless, very determined"

HIGHS

January: South Bank Show Awards – wins Best Pop Act

February: BRIT Awards – wins Best Female Solo Artist; *Elle* Style Awards – wins Best British Music Act

May: Ivor Novello Awards – wins Best Contemporary Song ('Rehab'); marries Blake Fielder-Civil in Miami

June: takes Glastonbury by storm…

September: Nationwide Mercury Award – nominated

September: Popjustice £20 Music Prize – wins Best British pop single of the year award ('Rehab')

September: working on a new album; performs at the Mercury Music Awards

September: rumours that she will record the theme tune for the next Bond film

September: MOBOs – wins Female Artist of the Year; Vodafone Live Music Awards – wins Best Female Artist

October: Q Awards – wins Best Album (*Back to Black*)

November: MTV Awards – nominated for Most Addictive Track ('Rehab') and Album of the Year

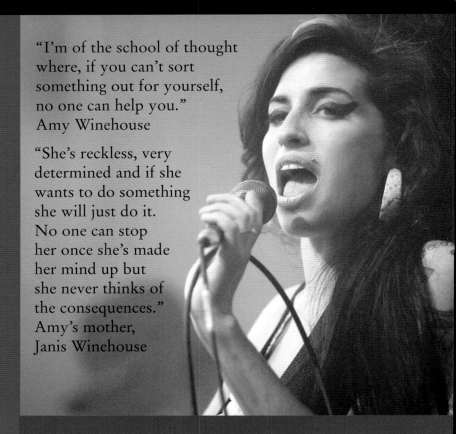

"I'm of the school of thought where, if you can't sort something out for yourself, no one can help you."
Amy Winehouse

"She's reckless, very determined and if she wants to do something she will just do it. No one can stop her once she's made her mind up but she never thinks of the consequences."
Amy's mother, Janis Winehouse

AMY'S

YEAR

LONDON

Kate Nash, a Londoner who found her way to fame from a MySpace fanbase, is the newest shining star in the tell-it-like-it-is generation.

She was born in 1987, in Harrow. She wanted to be an actress, but after being rejected by the Bristol Old Vic Theatre School she found solace in songwriting, and soon found her her fanbase on MySpace. *NME* has dubbed her music 'chavtronica': funky beats and an electro-charged feel accompanying witty insights into teen life, all delivered in a heavy but charming London accent.

Nash is an ardent supporter of the Save Camden Stables Market campaign. Planners are hoping to knock down the quirky, iconic market in north London to make way for a faceless mega-mall. Nash performed at an awareness-raising evening during the summer,

saying: "This is London and we shouldn't let other people change the place where we live." If the Market disappeared, "where would I buy my clothes?"

In February, her debut double A side single 'Caroline's a Victim' and 'Birds' reached No. 151 in the official UK Chart. In March she was signed to Fiction Records, part of Polydor. Her single 'Foundations' reached No. 2 in June in the official UK Chart, and in August her debut album *Made of Bricks* reached No. 1. She rounded off the year with a Q Award for Best Breakthrough Artist. Hailed as Lily Allen's natural successor, all eyes will be on Nash and her odd but hypnotic music in 2008.

"Her simple reflections capture the essence of teenage London life."
Vogue magazine

CALLING

Londoner Lily Allen's refreshingly cheeky attitude has ensured that she remains a media favourite. She was scarcely out of the gossip columns in 2007.

SCANDAL: On 5 August Allen was detained at Los Angeles Airport for five hours and questioned over an alleged assault on a photographer in London in March. It was reported that her US working visa had been revoked, though her manager denied this.

CANCELLATIONS: In August Allen cancelled several European festival appearances; she assured her fans on her MySpace page that sinusitis and strep throat had forced her to rest.

FASHION: On 9 May she launched her capsule collection 'Lily Loves' at fashion chain New Look.

SELF-IMAGE: Allen wrote on her MySpace blog that she felt "fat and ugly" and was considering plastic surgery. She subsequently apologised for the outpouring after an overwhelming response from worried fans.

AWARDS: BRIT Awards nominated: Best British Single ('Smile'), Best British Album (*Alright, Still*), Best British Female, Best British Breakthrough Act ('Smile'). **NME Awards:** Won Worst Dressed. Nominated: Best Solo Artist, Sexiest Woman, Worst Album (*Alright, Still*). **MTV Awards:** Nominated Best New Artist. **Q Awards:** Nominated Best Video ('Alfie').

SINGLES 2007: 5 March: 'Alfie' reached No. 15 in UK Singles Chart (upon hearing this song, her brother Alfie threw her laptop out of a window in revenge!). 16 July: 'Oh my God' was released – reached No. 12 in the UK (downloads only); in its second week it jumped to No.8.

"I'm flattered that the papers think I'm interesting, but they're turning me into a caricature."

Lily Allen

THE BOYS ARE BACK

The boy band sensation of the early 1990s, with eight chart-topping singles, were the first band since The Beatles to score four consecutive number ones. After ten years away, they reformed in 2006 and have gone from strength to strength in 2007.

After their momentous split in 1996, Take That disappeared from view – apart, that is, from Robbie Williams' rise to superstardom.

In 2006, they re-surfaced with The Ultimate Tour (minus Robbie) and the No. 1 single 'Patience' (the group's ninth No. 1), and rounded off the year with a No. 1 spot for the album *Beautiful World*. The stage was set for a triumphant year and 2007 did not disappoint.

TAKE THAT'S YEAR

FEBRUARY: Performed at the BRIT Awards, won Best British Single award for 'Patience'; it re-entered the Top Ten after 16 weeks in the charts

MARCH: Celebrated tenth No. 1 with 'Shine'

JUNE: 'I'd Wait for Life' single reached No. 17

JULY: Performed at Concert for Diana

OCTOBER: Appeared as the faces of M&S's Autograph range. Beautiful World Tour began. 'Rule the World' due for release – the theme song for the film *Stardust*. It stands as 3/1 bookies' favourite to win the Oscar for Best Original Song at the 2008 ceremony

156

FRIENDS REUNITED

The 'girl power' phenomenon of the late 1990s took the charts
by storm. But marriage, motherhood, solo careers and squabbles
all took their toll, and the band finally split in 2001. In 2007,
they announced that they were back in business.

A lot of water has passed under the bridge since the Spice Girls burst on to the scene with 'Wannabe' in 1996.

After releasing three studio albums and ten singles, selling in excess of 53 million records worldwide, the girls went their separate ways in 2001 to concentrate on solo careers.

On 28 June 2007 they reformed and are now planning a greatest hits album, plus an eleven-date tour, The Return of the Spice Girls, kicking off in Vancouver on 2 December 2007.

An official documentary of the band is to be made (release date as yet undisclosed). Geri Halliwell says: "You are going to get to know what is behind the stories that you've heard, it's going to be the most honest story you've ever heard, you're going to get to see the dark side of the Spice Girls, the gritty side, the tears."

Girl Power: "A self-reliant attitude among girls and young women
manifested in ambition, assertiveness and individualism." *OED*, 2001

"I don't want to play Glastonbury on the Sunday night in the pouring rain, which is what The Who did this year... You've got to pick your slot."

Mick Jagger

FESTIVAL FEVER

With more festivals than ever before, 2007 saw fans braving bad weather to witness some historic sets by legendary artists.

"We waited a long time to come here... Thanks for sticking with us."

Pete Townshend

FESTIVAL HIGHLIGHTS

8–10 June: The Rolling Stones played their first UK festival for more than 30 years on the Isle of Wight. They crossed the water on a privately chartered ferry.

22–24 June: Dame Shirley Bassey braved the mud in diamond-encrusted wellies at Glastonbury. The Who played the closing set.

6–8 July: Festival-goers faced 12-mile tailbacks at T in the Park at Balado, Kinross, Scotland. When they arrived, organisers were forced to close car parks due to muddy conditions.

18–19 August: Pete Doherty of Babyshambles threw his guitar into the crowd during their set at the V Festival in Chelmsford.

24–26 August: Music fans got down and dirty at The Carling Weekend: Reading and Leeds Festival. Waterlogged camping areas were closed and the car park was turned into a campsite. The Red Hot Chili Peppers were allegedly paid £4 million to perfom.

5–7 September: Primal Scream's Bestival set on the Isle of Wight was interrupted when Madness's Suggs stormed on stage.

MUDFEST

22–24 June
Glastonbury Festival

The 900-acre site became a mudbath after heavy rain.
Some 180,000 revellers found various ways to cope,
from using rubber dinghies to just wallowing in the
quagmire. Wellington boots sold for £80.

"It's gone very well, in spite of the rain and in
spite of the mud... Someone called me from Spain
and said they would swap all the sun they had
for the Glastonbury culture." Michael Eavis

7/7/7: LIVE EARTH
24-hour seven-continent concert series

The Live Earth concerts aimed to encourage action against climate change by raising public awareness. Concerts were staged in New York, Tokyo, Johannesburg, Shanghai, Rio de Janeiro, Sydney, Hamburg and London's Wembley Stadium.

"Live Earth doesn't have a final goal. I would only organise this if I could go on stage and announce concrete environmental measures from the American presidential candidates, Congress or major corporations. They haven't got those guarantees. So it's just an enormous pop concert."
Sir Bob Geldof

"We hope Live Earth will launch a global campaign giving a critical mass of people around the world the tools they need to help solve the climate crisis, but ultimately, corporations and governments must become global leaders taking decisive action to stop global warming."
Al Gore, former US vice-president, winner of the Nobel Peace Prize 2007

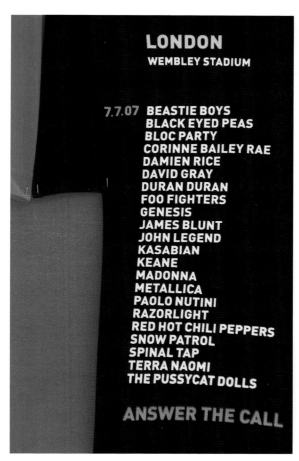

LONDON
WEMBLEY STADIUM

7.7.07　**BEASTIE BOYS**
BLACK EYED PEAS
BLOC PARTY
CORINNE BAILEY RAE
DAMIEN RICE
DAVID GRAY
DURAN DURAN
FOO FIGHTERS
GENESIS
JAMES BLUNT
JOHN LEGEND
KASABIAN
KEANE
MADONNA
METALLICA
PAOLO NUTINI
RAZORLIGHT
RED HOT CHILI PEPPERS
SNOW PATROL
SPINAL TAP
TERRA NAOMI
THE PUSSYCAT DOLLS

ANSWER THE CALL

LIVE EARTH: TAKING A STAND

Madonna closed the London concert with 'Hey You', a song inspired by the climate change campaign.

The concerts were criticised because of the carbon emissions created by the shows.

The BBC's average viewing ratings for the concerts only reached 3.1 million; the Concert for Diana the week before attraced some 11.4 million viewers.

The 70,000 tickets for the London concert were allocated by public ballot, and cost £55 each.

ABOVE: Simon Le Bon of Duran Duran BELOW: Kasabian

CONCERT FOR DIANA

1 July: William and Harry hosted a concert at Wembley Stadium to celebrate the life of Diana, Princess of Wales, on what would have been her 46th birthday.

The six-hour show began at 4 p.m., with cloudy wet weather failing to dampen the spirits of the 60,000-strong crowd, who were treated to an eclectic mix of performers. The line-up also featured the English National Ballet, a medley of Andrew Lloyd Webber songs, Ricky Gervais, guest speakers and recorded messages from Nelson Mandela, Bill Clinton and Tony Blair.

The concert was the brainchild of the two princes, who together closed the event with a tribute to their mother. Proceeds were shared equally between charities chosen by the princes and the Diana, Princess of Wales Memorial Fund. In the UK some 15 million people watched at home. The concert was also broadcast to over 500 million homes in 140 countries.

PERFORMERS INCLUDED

Sir Elton John Duran Duran James Morrison
Lily Allen Fergie The Feeling Pharrell Williams
Nelly Furtado Status Quo Joss Stone
Roger Hodgson Orson Will Young P. Diddy
Sir Tom Jones and Joe Perry Natasha Bedingfield
Bryan Ferry Anastacia KanYe West Take That

"For us, this has been the most perfect way of remembering her. And this is how she would want to be remembered." Prince William

TREND 2007: CROCS

The most unlikely fashion hit of the year?

Crocs have hit the headlines, not only for being the most unusual fashion footwear since the Ugg boot, but because of the dangers they can pose.

There was huge debate over the safety and levels of hygiene of the popular footwear, which is much favoured by nurses and hospital workers.

The malfunction of equipment at a Swedish hospital was blamed on static electricity allegedly created by the brightly-coloured clogs. It was claimed that the shoes were at risk of causing a 'cloud of lightning'.

In the UK, the Sheffield Teaching Hospitals Foundation Trust suggested banning the footwear in its hospitals too, saying that the shoes are unhygienic and cause a health and safety risk.

There were plenty of other 'Croc-horror' stories, many of which involved children injuring themselves while wearing the oversized shoes. One child reportedly had their foot sucked into an escalator.

> "You either love or hate the design but no one can say they're uncomfortable."
>
> Crocs spokesperson

CROC FACTS

Crocs were started in 2002 by two sailors who were looking for the perfect deck shoe.

20 million pairs of Crocs have been sold worldwide in the last 12 months.

They are made of a spongy foam resin (a trademarked substance called Croslite), not plastic.

Crocs are currently sold in more than 80 countries.

They are available in 17 eye-catching colours.

Celebrity fans include Jack Nicholson, Teri Hatcher, Al Pacino, Adam Sandler and George Bush.

The company manufactures around 5 million pairs of the shoes a month.

The shoes are stain-proof, odour-resistant, slip-resistant, have non-marking soles and they float.

The 'winter' Croc, a cosy waterproof, fleece-lined version of the shoe, is set to outsell the Ugg.

ECO FASHION

8 a.m., 25 April: 'I'm Not a Plastic Bag' – the limited edition Anya Hindmarch bag – was launched in Sainsbury's across the UK. All 20,000 bags sold out within an hour and were soon in demand by eco fashion fans and celebrities alike.

20,000 bags were available in 450 Sainsbury's stores for just £5, but stocks were limited to 30 per store and only one per customer.

The sold-out bags fetched up to £200 on eBay.

The project was criticised because the bags were manufactured in China and made of non-Fairtrade cotton. They were, however, carbon offset, non-profit making and complied with all aspects of Chinese Labour Law, according to the organisers.

The bags were also released in the USA and Asia but, following stampedes of fans trying get hold of one, some of the Asian launches were cancelled due to 'concerns' over customer safety.

"We want people to decline plastic bags wherever possible... We can make it cool for people to do the right thing and fashion gives people a platform to do that... we've had every actress and model on the phone about it. I love it, because it shows people do give a damn."

Anya Hindmarch

"We used to build civilisations.
Now we build shopping malls." Bill Bryson

RETAIL RIOTS

Savvy shoppers have voted with their feet. They have discarded expensive designer labels in favour of High Street bargains, and when supplies are low, or queues are long, tempers have become frayed.

27 March: Boots

Boots' £16.75 anti-aging 'No7 Protect & Perfect Serum' sold out nationwide within hours after it was featured on BBC's *Horizons* programme on 27 March. The following day, with sales up 2,000 per cent, 13 bottles sold every minute and riots were reported in Yorkshire when one woman bought the entire stock of her local store. In some branches, customers were limited to three pots each or put on waiting lists which reached 50,000. When new stocks reached the shops on 4 May, Boots stores were besieged by queues of shoppers. A factory in Nottingham had been working round the clock to pump out 24,000 bottles a day.

"At both basic science and clinical levels Boots No7 Protect & Perfect has been shown scientifically to repair photo-aged skin and improve the fine wrinkles associated with photo-ageing." Professor Griffiths, Foundation Professor of Dermatology, Manchester University

5 April: Primark

"It doesn't have to be expensive – Primark is just as good as Gucci." Trinny Woodall

Due to open at 10 a.m., managers werer forced to bring forward the opening of the new flasghip store by 15 minutes because a dangerous crush was developing outside. False rumours had been spread that all items would be given away for £1 and some dedicated fans had been queuing since 2 a.m.

Extra security staff were on duty to handle the hordes of shoppers. When the doors opened, shoppers were knocked to the ground in the frantic stampede to snatch a bargain.

Bargains included £8 jeans, a £2 bikini, £3 cotton T-shirts and a £22 cashmere cardigan.

Eventually a one-in, one-out policy was adopted, and people queuing waited more than two hours to get into the store.

"I have always been a huge fan of Topshop. I chose to work with them because they would be able to interpret my ideas and designs the right way."

Kate Moss

TOP OF THE SHOPS

8 p.m., 30 April: Topshop Oxford Street
launched Kate Moss's hotly anticipated range.

There was a huge sense of excitement before the launch, and over a thousand people flocked to Topshop's flagship Oxford Street store. Moss – who was reportely paid £3 million – posed briefly in the store's windows before the doors opened.

The clothes went on sale at Topshop's 225 UK outlets the next day, Tuesday 1 May. Shoppers seemed unanimous in their approval – an affordable collection of Moss's greatest hits, including waistcoats, hot pants, copies of vintage dresses and gladiator sandals.

4 September Odeon Leicester Square, London: Keira Knightley in a Rodarte gown, with Bulgari and Chanel jewellery, at the UK premiere of *Atonement*.

THE RED CARPET

25 February Oscars: Kate Winslet in a Valentino dress and Chopard jewellery.

5 June GLAMOUR Women of the Year Awards: Victoria Beckham steals the show in Chanel.

11 February BAFTAs: Sienna Miller arrives in a vintage Ungaro gown.

25 February Oscars: Emily Blunt poses for the cameras in a sparkling Calvin Klein dress.

11 February BAFTAs: Thandie Newton arrives wearing a dress by British designer Giles Deacon.

25 February Oscars: Rachel Weisz in a Vera Wang dress and vintage Cartier jewellery.

175

THE SWEETEST SCENT

More than 30 celebrities launched perfumes in 2007,
including the Beckhams, Kate Moss,
Hilary Duff and Gwen Stefani.

"This year has been the year of the celebrity scent, with more celebrities than ever putting their names to perfumes and aftershaves which promise to re-create a small part of their lifestyle as an aspiration for their admirers and fans."
Julia Bolsom, Head of Marketing, The Perfume Shop

KATIE PRICE: STUNNING
"I'm sure when women wear it, it will turn their men on. When I wear it, Peter can't keep his hands off me!"

SHILPA SHETTY: S2
"S2 represents where I am on a global scale and my family in India... This is a scent that comes from my heart."

JADE GOODY
Jade Goody's fragance Shh... was withdrawn from the shelves of The Perfume Shop's 134 stores in January following the *Celebrity Big Brother* race allegations. The perfume was launched in 2006 and immediately became a best seller.

"I don't want to put my face on the box. That would put everyone off."
Jade Goody

COLEEN MCLOUGHLIN: COLEEN X
"It's every girl's dream to have her own beauty range and that dream has come true."

KYLIE MINOGUE: DARLING AND SWEET DARLING
"The launch of my new fragrance coincides with a new chapter of my life."

SPORT

"you get big runs simply by batting"

"a phenomenon the like of which I have never seen before"

"England are looking forward rather than looking back"

"I think I'm a special one"

OPEN AT
LAST...

17 March: The new Wembley opens, after many delays

BIGGER AND BETTER

1 km: the circumference of the stadium

11 acres: the size of the new roof

52 metres: the height the stadium roof rises to above the pitch

133 metres: the height of the arch

315 metres: the span of the arch, making it the world's longest single span roof structure

2,618 toilets: estimated to be more than any other building in the world

£757 million: the final cost of the stadium

90,000 seats: making Wembley the largest football stadium in the world with every seat under cover

THE FOOTBALL SEASON 2006/07

Ask any two football fans to tell you about the football season at its end and you'll have two unique stories; one person's misery is another's unbridled joy.

by Gabby Logan

The 2006/07 season finished with Sir Alex Ferguson's ninth Premiership trophy and Manchester United restored as champions after one of their longest periods away from the top spot since the great Scotsman took over 21 years ago. Not so long ago yet another United Premiership title would have brought groans from the neutral, but for once there seemed to be a certain amount of satisfaction that it was United and not the expensively assembled Chelsea who took the title. Football fans are fickle if nothing else.

So the journey to the title seems a good place to start. Sir Alex Ferguson's squad looked well balanced and exciting from the start, but what none of us could predict was how lucky they would be when it came to injury. When Sir Alex worried that he was lacking strength in depth behind his two main strikers, he brought in the massively experienced Henrik Larsson for a four-month loan spell. But there were very few high profile long-term injuries and, as a result, there was a consistency which United haven't been able to produce for a few years.

The player of the season for both United and the Premiership as a whole was Ronaldo. The Portuguese winger had a sensational season which was all the more remarkable because it came off the back of a controversial World Cup encounter with Wayne Rooney; Ronaldo's involvement in his United team mate's sending off led many to believe that Ronaldo could be on his way out. On Ronaldo's return to the UK the pair obviously kissed and made up, and he seemed to mature in every area of his game. The PFA, which is the award the players seem to value the most as it is voted for by the players themselves, voted Ronaldo both the Player and Young Player of the Year.

If Ronaldo was the star man it should also be noted that the PFA Team of the Year had eight United players on the team sheet, including Paul Scholes who came back from an eye injury to have one of his vintage years. And, while we are talking about vintage players, Ryan Giggs, now in his 33rd year, looked as lively as ever and won his first ever Player of the Month award. United also had their best run in Europe for four years, losing out to the eventual winners AC Milan in the semi-finals. However, it was the home leg against Roma in the quarter-finals that many consider to be one of the most scintillating nights of football ever played at Old Trafford.

Jose Mourinho's team never gave up the fight in the league, but it was a season where they were always behind and after August they never made it to the top spot again. In February, Manchester United were nine points clear and seemingly cruising to the title, but just a month later they succumbed to defensive injuries and there was a last gasp effort by Chelsea to capitalise – in the end it was too little too late.

If United were relatively lucky with injuries then Chelsea were the opposite. Their captain and talisman John Terry missed a large portion of the season through injury, and the statistics show that Chelsea suffered without him. If that wasn't bad enough for Mourinho, a freak accident was to rob him of his keeper for the best part of three months. When Petr Cech collided with Stephen Hunt at Reading in October, the goal keeper was left with a depressed fracture of the skull. At the time many experts thought he would take at least six months to return; it's a testament to his determination that Cech was back three months later to start against Liverpool on 20 January. After that game he went on to keep a clean sheet for 810 minutes, emphasising just what a huge loss he had been.

One of the highlights for Jose Mourinho was the goal-scoring prowess of Didier Drogba, whose tally was 33 goals in all competitions, twice as many as the previous two seasons; he was top scorer in the Premiership with 20 goals. Michael Essien should also be singled out for praise: his play making and versatility on the pitch in both attack and defence allowed others to shine. Things didn't go much better for Jose in the Champions League. Not only did Chelsea go out at the first knock-out stage, they went out to Mourinho's old club, Porto.

Liverpool manager Rafa Benitez seems to be able to navigate his way around the Champions League with ease, reaching the second final in his three-year reign. Sadly for Liverpool it was time for AC Milan to take revenge for the famous 2005 victory, and in the end they beat their old adversaries 2-1. In the league Liverpool finished third, but on level points with Arsenal. It was disappointing for both sets of fans that they were so far behind the top two; 15 points away from Chelsea.

> **One of the highlights for Jose Mourinho was the goal-scoring prowess of Didier Drogba, whose tally was 33 goals in all competitions.**

However, the main news for Liverpool this season was the takeover in February by two American businessmen. The Moores family agreed a £219 million sale to George Gillet and Tom Hicks after a consortium from Dubai had failed in their bid to buy the club in January. It was an unsettling period, but the new owners appeared to be more than silent investors, regularly attending games and making the right noises for the fans when it came to promising investment and also a new stadium. So far the union seems to be a happy one and optimism is high.

While Liverpool were acquiring their new owners, Arsenal were saying goodbye to a very influential vice chairman; David Dein was released by mutual consent after he supported a proposed takeover by American billionaire Stan Kroenke. It certainly was the season for takeovers and talk of takeovers. Even more upsetting for Arsenal fans was the departure of Thierry Henry to Barcelona. It was a transfer which had been mooted for some time; in fact after Arsenal's appearance in the 2006 Champions League Final against Barcelona many were surprised that the Frenchman had stayed. Arsène Wenger has been at Arsenal for eleven years now and he is adept at rebuilding. Henry's departure was a signal for yet more of that.

Away from the top four, one of the great surprises of the season was Steve Coppell's Reading. Those who had watched them closely in the Nationwide realised that they were a hard-working team who fought for every ball and gave little away. But most pundits had predicted a scrappy season where the Royals would

Carlos Tevez

Didier Drogba

Thierry Henry

be fighting for survival. They did fight, but in the end it was for a place in the Uefa Cup. They finished seventh – just one point off sixth place, which would have delivered them a European berth. Perhaps we should have read the signs from their first match against Middlesbrough, where they were 2-0 down and went on to win 3-2.

One of the most protracted sagas in Premiership history began a few months before the season started when it was announced that West Ham were buying two high profile Argentinian internationals. The difference in this transfer was that Javier Mashcerano and Carlos Tevez were owned not by a club but by a third party. As the season progressed it became clear that West Ham were in a relegation battle and in the January transfer window Mascherano signed for Liverpool. However that was only after the West Ham manager Alan Pardew had been sacked and former Charlton boss Alan Curbishley was given the job. In a very dramatic turn of events, Alan Pardew was then given the manager's job at Charlton and found

himself back in the relegation battle against his old club. Sadly he couldn't save Charlton, who were relegated a week before the end of the season after a home defeat to Tottenham Hotspur. Watford had been relegated a couple of weeks before that.

West Ham needed a victory at Old Trafford on the last day of the season to survive. United were already Champions and fielded a weaker squad than normal; West Ham still had to fight for the win and it was the controversial Tevez who struck gold. With his transfer still under investigation and the other teams in the relegation battle threatening legal action against the Premier League for not docking West Ham points, it was a bitter irony for the clubs eventually relegated. Sheffield United were the third team relegated and perhaps the angriest about the controversial Tevez transfer, with legal action still ongoing. And, just to cap it all, Tevez completed his protracted transfer to Manchester United over the summer. Whichever way you look at it, he's been dominating the headlines all season long.

185

FOOTBALL CHAMPIONS

2006–07 SEASON

Premiership: Manchester United

FA Cup: Chelsea

Football League Championship: Sunderland

Football League One: Scunthorpe

Football League Two: Walsall

Scottish Premier League: Celtic

The Scottish Cup: Celtic

Uefa Champions League: AC Milan

Uefa Cup: Sevilla

TOP LEFT: 29 April: Celtic win the Scottish Premier League. TOP RIGHT: 19 May: Chelsea beat Manchester United to win the FA Cup.
BELOW: 13 May: Manchester United win the Premier League.

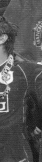

May: Jose Mourinho received a police caution after refusing to hand his dog over to animal welfare officials who wanted to put it in quarantine, fearing it had not had the necessary inoculations. The Yorkshire terrier later disappeared and was reportedly in Portugal.

"The dog is fine in Portugal. That big threat is away – you don't have to worry about crime anymore."
Jose Mourinho

July: Former England coach Sven-Goran Eriksson turned heads as boss of Premier League Man City, transforming the team overnight.

"It's always good to take on a job that's a challenge, and this is a great challenge for me."
Sven-Goran Eriksson

Arsène Wenger: with the loss of the charismatic Thierry Henry, coupled with the lack of any high profile signings, it seemed that Wenger and his beloved Arsenal might just be in meltdown. Yet within two months of the start of the 07/08 season, Arsenal – with an average age of 23 – were sitting, unbeaten, at the top the table.

OFF SIDE

Highs and lows on and off pitch...

Rooney gets off on right foot

After his World Cup 2006 debut was delayed by a broken metatarsal, Wayne Rooney's 2007/08 season got off to a bad start when he suffered a broken left foot. But on his 13 October return to England duty against Estonia he celebrated with his first goal for his country since Euro 2004.

Owen back on form

A thigh problem further hampered Michael Owen's recovery from the cruciate ligament injury that kept him out for the 2006/07 season. But, after missing Newcastle's opening fixtures, he went on to score five goals in as many games for club and country – including a brace against Russia and one against Israel. Then, cruelly struck down by a hernia, Owen made a scoring return for Newcastle just six days after surgery, before playing for England three days later.

England on the edge

Three successive 3-0 wins at the new Wembley appeared to have turned England's stuttering Euro 2008 qualifying campaign around. However, a disastrous 2-1 loss playing Russia on their plastic pitch on 17 October, left the team, at the time of writing, facing the prospect of failing to qualify for a major tournament for the first time since the 1994 World Cup.

Scotland resurgent

Scotland tore up the form book in their battle to qualify for Euro 2008. Drawn in the so-called 'group of death' alongside big name opponents France and Italy, they defied their critics with some eye-catching performances. The 1-0 victory against France was the highlight, and in players like James McFadden they have even greater hope for the future.

Profile: Jose Mourinho

Jose Mourinho, arriving as Chelsea manager on 2 June 2004, introduced himself with the confidence that would become his trademark. "Please don't call me arrogant, but I'm European champion and I think I'm a special one," he said, and, with that, he went on to shake up the hierarchy of English football.

Born in Setúbal, Portugal in 1963 as José Mário dos Santos Mourinho Félix to Portugal's then national goalkeeper, his professional career began as a coach, not a player. Stints as Sir Bobby Robson's translator at Sporting, FC Porto and then Barcelona led to success as a manager in Portugal, where he returned to guide unfashionable FC Porto to Uefa Cup success in 2003 before winning the Champions League the following year.

Recruited by Chelsea owner Roman Abramovich to deliver trophies, Mourinho's strategic skill returned a haul of two Premier League titles, the 2007 FA Cup, two League Cups, 2005's Community Shield and an unbeaten home record, making him Stamford Bridge's most successful manager ever. It came at a cost, though, as Mourinho splashed his owner's cash to the tune of over £187 million on new players, while his own rumoured yearly salary of £5 million made him football's highest paid manager.

Never shy of controversy, his reign was marked by clashes with officials, other managers – notably Arsenal's Arsène Wenger and Liverpool's Rafael Benítez – and Chelsea's boardroom. Yet after three seasons in charge, his departure from the club by mutual consent in September 2007 was met with angry demonstrations from fans and a tear from the manager as he admitted, "Yes, I cried. I've always had a relationship of love with the players and fans. I won't forget them and they won't forget me."

> "We have top players and, sorry if I'm arrogant, we have a top manager."
> Jose Mourinho

"If I wanted to have an easy job, I would have stayed at Porto – beautiful blue chair, the Uefa Champions League trophy, God, and after God, me."
Jose Mourinho on moving to England

"If he helped me out in training we would be bottom of the league and if I had to work in his world of big business, we would be bankrupt."
Jose Mourinho on Roman Abramovich

THREE WINNING YEARS

2 June 2004: appointed Chelsea manager

27 February 2005: Chelsea beat Liverpool 3–2 to win the Carling Cup

30 April 2005: beat Bolton 2–0 to win first Premier League title

29 April 2006: beat Man Utd 3–0 to win second Premier League title

27 February 2007: beat Arsenal 2–1 to win Carling Cup

19 May 2007: beat Man Utd 1–0 to win FA Cup

12 August 2007: beat Birmingham 3–2 to go 64 home games unbeaten – a Premier League record

19 September 2007: left Chelsea

RECORD-BREAKER

Under Mourinho, Chelsea played 185 games: won 124, drew 40 and lost 21

Chelsea's unbeaten home run under Mourinho was 67 games

Mourinho was Premier League Manager of the Year in both 2005 and 2006

Mourinho's trademark Armani overcoat was sold for £22,000 at a charity auction

Mourinho signed 21 players, costing in excess of £187 million

Mourinho's most expensive signing was Andriy Shevchenko at £31 million

His reported pay-off was £10 million

WHAT A DEBUT!

Lewis Hamilton looks set to keep us on the edge of our seats.

All eyes were on Lewis Hamilton in 2007 as the hopes of British racing brightened with the arrival of this polite, quietly determined 22-year-old. After all, there hasn't been a British champion for 10 years. But he's had a tough year.

With his McLaren team's alleged tactics resulting in disqualification from the Constructors Championship, and hostile rivalry with his team mate, Alonso, Hamilton has faced controversy at every turn. Yet he has become one of the greatest British sportsmen to emerge in recent years.

After leading the World Championship with 107 points going into the season's final race in São Paolo, on 21 October, he needed to finish fifth to claim the trophy. But a bad start and gearbox trouble robbed him of what would have been a fairytale end to his first season in Formula One. The future, though, is very bright indeed.

CHAMPION'S COUNTDOWN

1985: Born 7 January, Stevenage, Herts

1999: Signed to McLaren driver development support programme

2000: European karting champion. Moved on to racing cars the next year

2003: British Formula Renault Champion

2005: F3 Euroseries Champion

2006: GP2 Series champion

2007: First F1 drive for McLaren

2007: Autobiography published by HarperCollins (Hamilton received a reported seven-figure advance)

A STORY OF FIRSTS

First F1 rookie ever to earn a podium place in his first three races

Most consecutive podium finishes from debut race: 9

Most consecutive podium finishes for a British driver: 9 (equal with Jim Clark)

Youngest driver ever to lead the Drivers Championship, thrashing the record of Bruce McLaren

First driver to achieve consecutive wins from pole position in debut season

First black driver to compete in F1

Third youngest driver to achieve an F1 pole position

> "Lewis Hamilton is a phenomenon the like of which I have never seen before."
> Murray Walker

"To say it was magnificent would probably be an understatement." Brian Ashton

RUGBY WORLD CUP 2007

It was a Rugby World Cup that threw out the form book. England were supposed to be past it, the Southern hemisphere teams of Australia and the All Blacks were deemed to be too strong, too progressive and too good for their Northern hemisphere contemporaries, while the hosts, France, were expected to lift the famous Webb Ellis Trophy in Paris. In the end, all the predictions proved false.

Brian Ashton's defending champions had a worse start to the tournament than any previous defending champion in the history of the World Cup. Though they beat the USA in their first pool game, they were thrashed 36-0 by South Africa then limped to a 36-20 victory over Tonga. However, their 12-10 triumph over the Wallabies on 6 October was the shock of the competition until France edged to a 20-18 win against favourites New Zealand later that day. That defeat sealed New Zealand's worst-ever performance in the World Cup.

England's run was in stark contrast to those of the Welsh and Irish. Wins against Japan and Canada but a humbling defeat against Australia in Cardiff meant Wales needed to beat Fiji in order to progress to the knock-out stages. After an epic game, they lost 38-34 and went home with their tails between their legs while the knowledge that their thrilling game would go down in folklore was scant consolation.

Ireland fared even worse. Thought of as one of the Six Nations' stronger teams, their heavy losses against France and Argentina, after less than impressive victories against minnows Georgia and Namibia,

meant they also failed to progress from the group stages; a disaster for a nation with high expectations.

Scotland, meanwhile, played better than anyone could have forecast. In a tough group that included Italy and New Zealand, they battled through to the quarter-finals where they were narrowly beaten by the muscular Argentinians; a platform from which to build.

England, though, facing the Springboks in the Final stood on the threshold of greatness. A win against the team who had so humiliatingly thrashed them in the group stages would mean captin Phil Vickery's men would be the only team to successfully defend the Web Ellis trophy in its history. It would have been a remarkable journey.

In a game that is harder hitting, faster paced and more dynamic than ever before, the England team's reputation was already redeemed before they entered the Stade de France on 20 October. A win would have been the icing on the cake, but their brave display in losing 6-15, with a disallowed try the game's talking point, was enough to prove English rugby is again a force with which to be reckoned.

SIX NATIONS RUGBY

	Played	Won	Drawn	Lost	For	Against	Points
France	5	4	0	1	155	86	8
Ireland	5	4	0	1	149	84	8
England	5	3	0	2	119	115	6
Italy	5	2	0	3	94	147	4
Wales	5	1	0	4	86	113	2
Scotland	5	1	0	4	95	153	2

"One of the important things to have come from the Six Nations is that, for the first time in three years, England are looking forward rather than looking back."

Rob Andrew, Director of Rugby, England

3 February: the RBS 6 Nations tournament 2007 saw France crowned champions for the fourth time in six years.

France retained the Six Nations title without ever hitting top gear. Players such as Yannick Jauzion and Christophe Dominici had moments of brilliance, but the front five looked vulnerable. In the prescient words of the manager, Jo Maso, "For the moment we are champions of Europe… if we want to be world champions, we will have to be better than that."

Ireland were arguably the best team, scoring more tries than any of their opponents, but a lack of concentration in the closing seconds of their match against France at Croke Park probably cost them the championship.

Although England won three of their five matches, their performance was patchy, leaving considerable room for improvement, with newcomers David Strettle, Shane Geraghty, Toby Flood and Tom Rees all looking promising.

Wales looked as if they were heading for a Six Nations whitewash, but on the last Saturday of the championship they dug deep and defeated England, to the delight of crowds at Cardiff's Millennium Stadium, with James Hook an impressive newcomer. Because of that victory, it was Scotland who ended up with the wooden spoon.

Italy were the true success story of the championship. Their dramatic defeat of Scotland was their inaugural away win, and the entire pack has improved beyond recognition. Italy have truly arrived on the international scene.

PLAYERS OF THE CHAMPIONSHIP

Harry Ellis (England)

Gordon D'Arcy (Ireland)

James Hook (Wales)

Chris Paterson (Scotland)

Clement Poitrenaud (France)

Sergio Parisse (Italy)

THE FIELD

RUGBY UNION

After victory in the 2006/07 Premiership and the domestic cup against Gloucester and Ospreys respectively, Leicester were on course for an historic treble. But, in a memorable European final, Wasps won 25-9 to achieve Heineken Cup glory.

Guinness Premiership:
Leicester

EDF Energy Cup:
Leicester

Heineken Cup:
Wasps

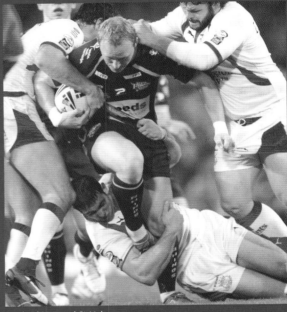

Leeds Rhinos and St Helens.

RUGBY LEAGUE

The competition between Leeds and St Helens dominated rugby league in 2007. Split by just a point in the Super League, Leeds romped home with the title after the Grand Final against Saints, who had to make do with the Challenge Cup.

Super League:
Leeds Rhinos

Challenge Cup:
St Helens

London Wasps captain Lawrence Dallaglio celebrates with his team

THE PITCH

The poor summer weather took its toll on the county season with several clubs – notably Worcestershire – forced to reschedule games away from their home grounds.

LV COUNTY CHAMPIONSHIP: SUSSEX

Sussex, the defending champions, pipped Lancashire to the County Championship after a thrilling season-long race came down to the wire. In the end, heartbroken Lancashire were 24 runs short of securing their first title in 73 years. "The lads are just broken," admitted tearful Lancashire captain Mark Chilton.

FRIENDS PROVIDENT TROPHY: DURHAM

Shane Warne's Hampshire were blown away by the bowling of Durham's Ottis Gibson in a rain-affected final at Lord's. It earned Durham a first major domestic title and left captain Paul Collingwood delirious, while his Australian counterpart fumed. "I hate losing, and this is right up there," said Warne.

NATWEST PRO40: WORCESTERSHIRE

In a season in which they were both relegated and their ground was hit by extreme flooding, Worcestershire's one highlight was their six wicket Pro40 final win over neighbours Gloucestershire. "We won't need any help celebrating," said their captain, Gareth Batty.

TWENTY20 CUP: KENT

Kent's victory over Gloucestershire was tinged with controversy after Kent skipper Robert Key was out to a catch that wasn't, and the umpires lost count of the balls bowled. But the result was never in doubt after Darren Stevens flayed the 13 required from the last over to win the cup, only their third domestic title in 29 years.

The Sussex team

The Worcestershire team celebrate

199

LONDON ON THE RUN

22 April: Unseasonable April sunshine and nearly 40,000 runners made for the hottest and biggest Marathon ever.

With temperatures reaching 21°C at midday, runners faced gruelling conditions. Organisers tried to help by setting up run-through showers, and extra water supplies and ambulance staff were at the ready.

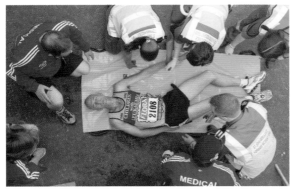

"It was like running in a desert today. I stopped to help one guy. It was quite bad. They were dropping like flies."
Gordon Ramsay

In the men's race, many had hoped for a win for double Olympic track champion Haile Gebrselassie, but the Ethiopian pulled out at the 20-mile mark with a stitch, leaving Kenyan Martin Lel to regain his title. In the women's race, Chunxiu Zhou became the first Chinese athlete to win the event, while the wheelchair races were won by a pair of Britons – David Weir and Shelly Woods.

LONDRES: LE GRAND DÉPART

6–8 July: The Tour de France was launched from London for the first time in its 100-year history.

More than two million spectators gathered in London as the capital hosted the *Grand Départ*, comprising the Opening Ceremony in Trafalgar Square and the Prologue stage of the race, beginning in Whitehall and taking in famous sights such as the Houses of Parliament, Westminster Abbey, Buckingham Palace, Wellington Arch and Hyde Park.

Fabian Cancellara of Switzerland raced down the Mall to win the Prologue in an incredible time of 8 minutes 50.74 seconds over the 7.9km course, finishing around 13 seconds in front of second-placed Andreas Kloden of Germany, while the USA's George Hincapie finished third. Great Britain's Bradley Wiggins, who grew up in London, came fourth. The following day, riders began Stage 1 of the Tour de France by cycling from London to Canterbury.

"My vision for London is a city where increasing levels of cycling will create a more sustainable transport system and improve the health of Londoners. I am certain that the Tour de France will inspire people to take up cycling."
Ken Livingstone, Mayor of London

THE CAPTAIN OF ALL CAPTAINS

7–11 June: When England won the third Test against the West Indies, it was Michael Vaughan's 21st victory as captain – more than any of his predecessors.

Vaughan's first full calendar year as captain was 2004, when his team were unbeaten, with a record eight consecutive victories and a series win against West Indies in the Caribbean for the first time since 1968. In 2005, he topped that when his team ended an 18-year drought against Australia to reclaim the Ashes.

"This moment is obviously special for me because I have passed a legend in Peter May. It is a huge honour for me to do that... But you don't win games of cricket without having good players and I've been very fortunate to have a lot of good players in my team."
Michael Vaughan

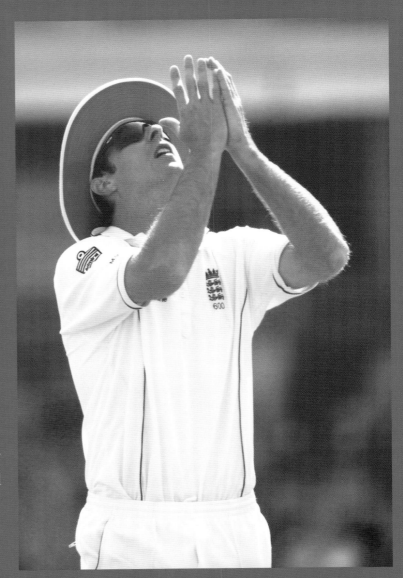

1,500 RUNS AND COUNTING...

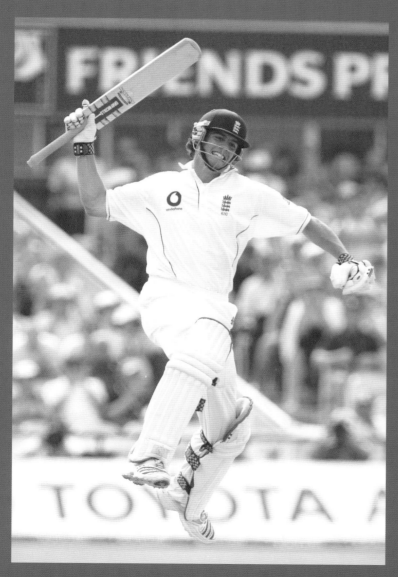

7–11 June: In the same match against the West Indies, 22-year-old Alastair Cook's total of 105 secured his sixth Test century, making him England's most prolific young batsman.

Don Bradman, Sachin Tendulkar and Javed Miandad are the only other men in Test history to have scored more hundreds at the same age.

Though his innings of 43 in the second Test against India in July was not a classic, it took him past the 1,500 Test runs milestone as the fastest Englishman to do so.

"Who knows where Cooky can go at such a young age?" Kevin Pietersen

"It may sound obvious but you get big runs simply by batting and not letting other things get to you." Alastair Cook

CRICKET WORLD CUP

It was the World Cup that nobody will forget, but for all the wrong reasons...

In theory, it was the perfect tournament – two months, from 13 March to 28 April, in glorious sunshine, packed out with the Caribbean's cricket-crazy fans. But it didn't quite work. High ticket prices meant that few locals could attend, leaving empty stadia. And what a lot of games there were – 51 over seven weeks. With only 16 teams involved from the start, there were also many repeat fixtures.

With Pakistan falling prey to Ireland, and India and New Zealand losing to Bangladesh, the group stages threw up some surprises. Yet Pakistan's swift return home also triggered the lowest point in international cricket – the death of their coach Bob Woolmer.

It was no shock that the teams in the final eight were Australia, New Zealand, Sri Lanka, South Africa, England, Ireland, Bangladesh and the West Indies. Yet England's inconsistent batting, toothless bowling and low run-rates completed their disappointing winter, ending Duncan Fletcher's tenure as coach. The West Indies' Brian Lara, one of the game's all-time greats, struggled to find form, and had difficulty coaxing performances from his men.

The semi-finalists were the best four teams in the tournament by some distance, with impressive individual displays. New Zealand's Scott Styris put in some dogged work with willow and leather; South Africa's Andrew Hall crushed England in the Super Eights with figures of 5–18; Sri Lanka slinger Lasith Malinga took an incredible four wickets in as many balls against South Africa, also in the Super Eights.

Finalists Sri Lanka looked well equipped to test Australia, the undisputed kings of one-day cricket, but Ricky Ponting's charges made light work of their rivals. They made 281–4 from a reduced 38 overs, with opening batsman Adam Gilchrist steaming to 149 from just 104 deliveries, setting Sri Lanka a recalculated target of 269 from 36 overs.

A rain-interrupted game ended in high farce, as darkness took hold of the Kensington Oval and it became apparent that the match officials were unsure of the rules on completing the game. Eventually it transpired that the green-and-golds won by 53 runs, but only after they had twice celebrated their victory.

The following day, a press conference was held so that ICC chief executive Malcolm Speed could apologise publicly for the chaos. As he began to speak, the hoarding behind him fell from the wall, almost hitting his head. A fittingly ignominious finish to a bizarre World Cup.

CRICKET TEST RESULTS
The West Indies and India in England

It was an altogether disappointing summer for England's Test cricket team. Beginning with a simple series win over a shockingly out-of-sorts West Indies, it ended with a rain-interrupted series defeat to India.

WEST INDIES IN ENGLAND

17–21 MAY: First Test, Lord's. Match drawn. England 553/5d and 284/8 declared; West Indies 437 and 89/0.

25–28 MAY: Second Test, Headingley. England won by an innings and 283 runs. England 570/7d; West Indies 146 and 141 (follow-on).

7–11 JUNE: Third Test, Old Trafford. England won by 60 runs. England 370 and 313; West Indies 229 and 394.

15–19 JUNE: Fourth Test, Chester-le-Street. England won by seven wickets. West Indies 287 and 222; England 400 and 111/3.
Players of the series: Shivnarine Chanderpaul (West Indies) and Monty Panesar (England).

1 JULY: First ODI, Lord's. England won by 79 runs. England 225 (49.5 overs); West Indies 146 (39.5 overs).

4 JULY: Second ODI, Edgbaston. West Indies won by 61 runs. West Indies 278/5 (50 overs); England 217 (46 overs).

7 JULY: Third ODI, Trent Bridge. West Indies won by 93 runs. West Indies 289/5 (50 overs); England 196 (44.2 overs).
Player of the series: Shivnarine Chanderpaul.

INDIA IN ENGLAND

19–23 JULY: First Test, Lord's. Match drawn. England 298 and 282; India 201 and 282/9.

27–31 JULY: Second Test, Trent Bridge. India won by 7 wickets. England 198 and 355; India 481 and 73/3.

9–13 AUGUST: Third Test, the Oval. Match drawn. India 664 and 180/6d; England 345 and 369/6.
Players of the series: James Anderson (England) and Zaheer Khan (India).

21 AUGUST: First ODI, the Rose Bowl. England won by 104 runs. England 288/2 (50 overs); India 184 (50 overs).

24 AUGUST: Second ODI, County Ground. India won by 9 runs. India 329/7 (50 overs); England 320/8 (50 overs).

27 AUGUST: Third ODI, Edgbaston. England won by 42 runs. England 281/8 (50 overs); India 239 (48.1 overs).

30 AUGUST: Fourth ODI, Old Trafford. England won by 3 wickets (with 12 balls remaining). India 212 (49.4 overs); England 213/7 (48 overs).

2 SEPTEMBER: Fifth ODI, Headingley. India won by 38 runs (Duckworth/Lewis method). India 324/6 (50 overs); England 242/8 (39 out of a reduced 39 overs).

5 SEPTEMBER: Sixth ODI, the Oval. India won by 2 wickets (with two balls remaining). England 316/6 (50 overs); India 317/8 (49.4 overs).

8 SEPTEMBER: Seventh ODI, Lord's. England won by 7 wickets (with 82 balls remaining). India 187 (47.3 overs); England 188/3 (36.2 overs).
Player of the match: Kevin Pietersen (England).
Player of the series: Ian Bell (England).

CHAMPIONS!

RUNNING AGAINST ADVERSITY

Christine Ohuruogu, 23, finished serving a twelve-month ban for missing three out-of-competition drug tests in August.

On 29 August at the World Athletics Championships in Osaka, Japan, she became the first British woman to win a world championship track event for 14 years.

In a heartstopping finish she beat her compatriot Nicola Sanders, who won silver, running her personal best at 49.61 seconds to take the 400m title.

"I trained, got up every day and did my work. I trained hard, always with the world championships in mind. It was all a dream."

In 2007 British champions led the world in several fields, and thrilled millions of fans.

SUPERBIKER

7 October: 26-year-old James Toseland captured his second World Superbike title on the French circuit at Magny Cours. Toseland, who rides for the Ten Kate Honda team, finished seventh in his first race and sixth in his second, but won the title because of his overall standings. He also won the title in 2004.

> "This is what I live for, this is the only thing that matters, getting this trophy."

BOXING STAR

Ricky Hatton, the boxer from Stockport, returned to the Light Welterweight class in 2007, after a spell at Welterweight. On 20 January he met Juan Ungaro in Las Vegas, winning in twelve rounds and recapturing the unified IBF and IBO Light Welterweight titles. On 23 June Hatton retained his title when he knocked out Mexico's Jose Luis Castillo in the fourth round.

He is due to meet Floyd Mayweather Jr in Las Vegas on 8 December. Tickets for this eagerly awaited fight sold out in just 35 minutes.

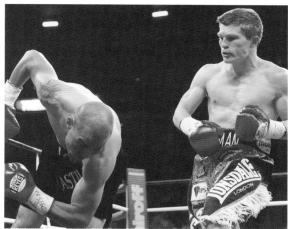

> "Ultimately my goal is Floyd Mayweather Jr. He's regarded as the best pound for pound fighter, so who wouldn't want to fight him?"

RUNNERS AND RIDERS

Grand National (14 April)

Irish eyes were smiling at the John Smith's Grand National, as 33/1 shot Silver Birch became the sixth Emerald Isle-trained winner in the last nine years.

Derby (2 June)

Frankie Dettori finally won the Derby at the 15th attempt, making it a clean sweep of career Classics. His mount Authorized secured him an emphatic victory, finishing five lengths clear.

> "I thought the whole world was shouting for me inside the final furlong. It was like an oil painting, it was all so beautifully smooth." Frankie Dettori

Ascot (19–23 June)

At Ascot, Yeats won his second consecutive Gold Cup in the showpiece event of the meeting on Ladies' Day. Ridden by Mick Kinane, the favourite became the tenth horse to win the race multiple times.

Goodwood (31 July–4 August)

Ryan Moore stole the show at Glorious Goodwood, with four wins on one day, including the King George Stakes on Moorhouse Lad and the feature race, the Goodwood Cup, on Allegretto.

25 June–8 July
WIMBLEDON

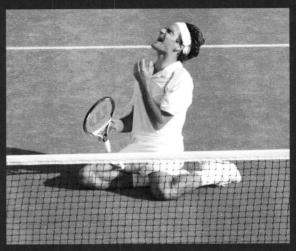

In the singles, Roger Federer took his fifth Wimbledon title in a row, beating Rafael Nadal, and a resurgent Venus Williams won the ladies' singles, overpowering Marion Bartoli.

It may have been Tim Henman's Wimbledon swansong, but his five-set first-round epic win over Carlos Moya was a classic. The British No. 2 could not repeat the feat, and was knocked out in the second round, after another five-set match against Feliciano Lopez. Henman played the final match of his career in the Davis Cup tie on 22 September 2007.

> "I was telling him, 'Jamie, let's go. This return, hit a good one because you are going to get many kisses'."
>
> Jelena Jankovic

What of the men's No. 1? Andy Murray was nursing a long-term wrist injury and did not compete in the tournament. It was his older brother, Jamie, who walked out on to Centre Court for a final, albeit in the mixed doubles, partnering Serbia's Jelena Jankovic. The flirtatious relationship between the pair triggered many headlines, as did their ultimate victory, beating the experienced Jonas Björkman and Alicia Molik by three sets to one.

DRAMA AT THE OPEN

22 July: Dubliner Padraig Harrington became the first Irishman to win the Open for 60 years and the first European to win a major since Paul Lawrie triumphed in 1999, also at Carnoustie.

35-year-old Harrington won the 136th Open Championship at Carnoustie, securing victory by just one stroke in a four-hole play-off with Sergio Garcia, who had led for the first three rounds. "To tell you the truth, I don't feel like I did anything wrong... I hit unbelievable puts. They just didn't go in," Garcia said. It was a good tournament for the Emerald Isle, as teenager Rory McIlroy collected the silver medal for the leading amateur.

Elsewhere on the men's tour, the USA's Tiger Woods picked up the PGA Championship (6–12 August), with his countryman Zach Johnson winning the Masters (2–8 April). Argentina's Angel Cabrera finished top of the pile in the other major of the year, the US Open (11–17 June).

On 27–30 September, Britain and Ireland retained the Seve Trophy after beating Continental Europe 8-2 in the singles to win 16½-11½. Nick Faldo captained the team to victory in the competition named after Seve Ballesteros, the continent's most successful golfer.

Tiger Woods celebrates winning the PGA Championship. He finished first on the PGA Tour seven times in 2007, and ranks first in Career Earnings on the PGA Tour.

"I think if I'd lost, it would have been very hard to take. If Sergio had parred the last and I'd lost, I think I would have struggled to come back and be a competitive golfer."

Padraig Harrington

FAREWELL

"I'm a ballsy, truth-telling... hell-raising activist"

"we might all be happier if we knew less"

"it also helped relieve all the anger"

"some make money and some make history"

DAME ANITA RODDICK

1942–2007

Controversial, entrepreneurial and unconventional, Dame Anita Roddick was perhaps Britain's most successful businesswoman. Her Body Shop empire spanned 55 countries, with 2,100 branches and amassed her a vast personal fortune. But it was her rejection of big-business's 'pin-striped dinosaurs' and embracing of green issues that secured her pioneering celebrity.

Born Anita Lucia Perilli in West Sussex in 1942, she was raised by her café-owning Jewish-Italian parents before becoming a teacher. As a '60s hippy she travelled the world before marrying her long-term business partner Gordon. By 1976 she had two daughters and had established the first Body Shop in Brighton with a £4,000 bank loan.

Within 10 years the company's informal style and ethical policies, alongside Roddick's flair for publicity, made The Body Shop a high-street staple. Its 1985 flotation on the stock market made Roddick the country's fourth richest woman. She used her wealth and fame to support campaigners such as CND, Amnesty International and Friends of the Earth, while also helping to launch *Big Issue* magazine.

In 2004, after selling her company for £652 million to cosmetics giant L'Oreal, she discovered that she had contracted Hepatitis C after the birth of her second daughter. It was to be a cause she would dedicate herself to for the rest of her life.

She was made OBE in 1988 and appointed Dame in 2003, and died in September of a stroke. She was 64.

"I'm a ballsy, truth-telling, free-thinking, heart-bleeding, myth-debunking, non-conforming and hell-raising activist."

JANE TOMLINSON

1964–2007

After being given six months to live in 2000, Jane Tomlinson's heroics over the following seven years are nothing short of astonishing. Her list of achievements are as inspirational as they are extraordinary, including raising £1.75m for charity (including her own Jane's Appeal) and competing in the world's most gruelling athletics events.

Diagnosed with cancer in 1991 aged 26, the Wakefield born mother of two underwent a mastectomy before beginning a diploma in radiography. The cancer was treated again three years later, but, after the birth of her third child in 2000, it returned, this time terminally.

"I decided to take control," she said, and in 2001 began a fundraising campaign that included running in April's London Marathon, an August triathlon, and October's Great North Run. In March 2003 she cycled 1,060 miles from John O'Groats to Land's End, despite undergoing chemotherapy twice on the ride. Days after completing the ride she ran the London Marathon again.

She also finished the New York marathon, cycled 2,500 miles across Europe, and remains the only person with incurable cancer to complete an Ironman contest – a feat she managed twice. Her final challenge, cycling 4,200 miles across America in June 2006, could only be achieved with the help of painkillers and morphine.

Tomlinson received many awards and was made an MBE in 2003 and a CBE in 2007. She died, aged 43, on 3 September.

"The running was a way of showing I could still do something positive. It also helped relieve all the anger, the sense that this was so unfair and why was it happening to me."

LORD DEEDES

1913–2007

He was a war hero, Conservative MP and cabinet minister, but it was as a journalist and editor that Lord Deedes – or Bill as he preferred to be called – was most renowned. Colleagues remember his endearing personality and self-deprecation as fondly as his trademark luminous socks and cigarette holder, but his amiable old-buffer image, reinforced by his immortalisation as *Private Eye*'s Dear Bill, masked one of Britain's most acute newsmen.

Born in 1913, William Francis Deedes began his career in 1931 on the *Morning Post*. Alongside novelist Evelyn Waugh, he then covered the Abyssinian war for the *Daily Mail* – and inspired the character of William Boot in Waugh's 1938 novel *Scoop*. After serving in the King's Rifle Corps in World War Two, in which he won the Military Cross, he became a legendary *Telegraph* columnist.

In 1954, he joined Churchill's government as a junior minister and, by 1962, was asked to sit in Macmillan's cabinet. In 1974, aged 61, he became the editor of *The Daily Telegraph* and thus cemented his legend. There his genteel nature and characteristic mixed metaphors – dubbed 'Billisms' – were a calming influence until his 1986 ousting.

A close friend of Denis and Margaret Thatcher, 'The Grand Old Man of Fleet Street', as he was known, continued to write incisive editorial, often from war-zones, until the week before his death and, astonishingly, was named British Press Awards' Reporter of the Year at the age of 84.

He was made life peer, becoming Baron Deedes, in 1986 and was appointed KBE in 1999. He died in August, aged 94.

"We might all be happier if we knew less about what was going on in the world."

TONY WILSON

1950–2007

It's been said that without Tony Wilson there would have been no music scene in Manchester: no Joy Division, no Happy Mondays, no Madchester. As the maverick ringmaster of the nascent '80s clubbing culture there, he put the city, pop-culturally, on the map.

Born in Salford in 1950, he moved from grammar school to Cambridge where he edited the Jesus College newspaper. It led to an early career as a journalist and, by 1973, his charm had earned him presenting work on Granada's *World In Action* and music show *So It Goes*.

It was there that he became synonymous with Manchester music, booking the Sex Pistols for the programme before setting up the legendarily haywire Factory Records in 1978, run according to Wilson's socialist principles. There he signed an influential crop of post-punk bands who, in turn, led him to dance music. This he capitalised on by opening the Haçienda nightclub – as renowned for its pioneering music as it was for drugs and mismanagement. Its clubbers witnessed the birth of house music in the UK, and performances by New Order, The Smiths, The Stone Roses, Oasis and even Madonna before it closed in 1997.

Both arrogant and engaging, his immortalisation in the film *24 Hour Party People*, in which he was played by comedian Steve Coogan, appealed to his sense of self-promotion and celebrity, but masked his more serious political quests for success in local government in the North.

He died on 10 August, at the age of 57, following complications from kidney cancer.

"I am famous for being the only person who didn't make any money out of the Manchester music scene of the 80s and 90s. I used to say: some make money and some make history – which is very funny until you find you can't afford to keep yourself alive."

ALAN BALL
1945–2007

At 5ft 6ins, Alan Ball was told he would never become a professional footballer. But his ability and work rate brought success at Blackpool, Everton, Arsenal and Southampton over two decades before a managerial career. It was his performances in England's midfield, for whom he earned 72 caps, that sealed his legend. The youngest player during England's 1966 World Cup win, he was also named Man of the Match for his combative but dazzling play. He died of a heart attack, aged 61.

COLIN McRAE
1968–2007

In 1995, Scotsman Colin McRae became the youngest driver, and first Briton, to win the World Rally Championship, and from there he went on to enjoy stratospheric success. Rallying's first superstar, his driving was full-throttle and he became a household name after sales of the PlayStation game 'Colin McRae Rally' hit the eight million mark. His final rally win at 2002's Safari Rally, his 25th victory, made him the sport's then most successful driver. He died in a helicopter crash, aged 39.

IN MEMORIAM

Ingmar Bergman (1918–2007) film director

Isabella Blow (1958–2007) editor and style icon

Alan Coren (1938–2007) humourist and broadcaster

Charles Forte, Lord Forte (1908–2007) businessman

Bruce Hay (1950–2007) rugby player

Ronnie Hazlehurst (1928–2007) composer

Frankie Laine (1913–2007) singer

Joe Mitty (1919–2007) founder of Oxfam

Bernard Manning (1930–2007) comedian

Marcel Marceau (1923–2007) mime artist

George Melly (1926–2007) jazz veteran

Anna Nicole Smith (1967–2007) model and actress

Luciano Pavarotti (1935–2007) opera singer

Ian Porterfield (1946–2007) footballer and manager

Mike Reid (1940–2007) comedian and actor

Ian Richardson (1934–2007) actor

Baron Guy de Rothschild (1909–2007) banker

Tony Ryan (1936–2007) founder of Ryanair

Derek Shackleton (1924–2007) cricketer

Sidney Sheldon (1917–2007) novelist

Ned Sherrin (1931–2007) broadcaster and writer

Kurt Vonnegut Jr (1922–2007) novelist

Bob Woolmer (1948–2007) sportsman

Boris Yeltsin (1931–2007) politician

William Young (1900–2007) airman, last known
remaining WW1 veteran of the Royal Flying Corps

Boris Yeltsin

Anna Nicole Smith

Mike Reid

Isabella Blow

PICTURE CREDITS

Contents
4–5 left to right Carl Rose/Rex Features, AP/PA Photos, Ray Tang/Rex Features, PA Photos
6–7 left to right Tom Stoddart/Getty Images, UK Press/PA Photos, Ian Watton/Getty Images, Rex Features

The Year Of…
10–11 left to right Chris Jackson/Getty Images, Matt Cardy/Getty Images, PA Archive/PA Photos
12 Carl Rose/Rex Features
14 PA Archive/PA Photos
15 clockwise from top Chris Jackson/Getty Images, PA Wire/PA Photos, Chris Jackson/Getty Images
16 Chris Jackson/Getty Images
19 left to right, top to bottom c.Sony Pictures/Everett/Rex Features, Jeff J Mitchell/Getty Images, Jonathan Hordle/Rex Features, PA Archive/PA Photos, Jonathan Hordle/Rex Features, Rex Features, Rex Features, AFP/Getty Images
20–21 Jim Dyson/Getty Images
22–23 Matt Cardy/Getty Images
24–25 Peter Macdiarmid/Getty Images
27 Lars Baron/Getty Images
28 Ray Roberts/Rex Features
34–35 left to right Heather Perry/Getty Images, PA Wire/PA Photos, 24/7 Media/Rex Features, Rex Features

People in the News
36–37 from left to right PA Archive/PA, EMPICS Entertainment/PA, AP/PA Photos
38–39 Pool/Getty Images
40 Dave Hogan/Getty Images
41 Dave M Bennett/Getty Images
43 from top to bottom Joe Raedle/Getty Images, AFP/PA Photos
44 Sebastian Meyer/Getty Images
45 Leon Neal/Getty Images
46 AP/PA Photos
47 left to right PA Wire/PA Photos, PA Archive/PA Photos, PA Wire/PA Photos
48 AP/PA Photos
49 clockwise from top left Most Wanted/Rex Features, Sipa Press/Rex Features, Alex Oliveira/Rex Features, Rex USA Ltd/Rex Features, Offside/Rex Features, Stewart Cook/Rex Features
50–51 Stan Honda/Getty Images
52–53 left to right PA Archive/PA Photos, PA Wire/PA Photos, PA Wire/PA Photos, AP/PA Photos
54–55 from left to right Rex Features, Mark Campbell/Rex Features, Jamie Jones/Rex Features, PA Wire/PA Photos
56 clockwise from middle left Excel Media/Rex Features, PAWire/PA Photos, Matt Cardy/Getty Images, PA Archive/PA Photos
57 left Sipa Press/Rex Features, top middle Scott Meyers/Rex Features bottom middle EMPICS Sport/PA Photos right ABACA/PA Photos
58 EMPICS Entertainment/PA Photos
59 top Brian Rasic/Rex Features bottom Rex Features

Showbiz and Media
60–61 left to right Huw John/Rex Features, Ray Tang/Rex Features, Rex Features
63 John Swannell
65 Nils Jorgensen/Rex Features
66 Ray Tang/Rex Features
67 MJ Kim/Getty Images
68 top left Phil Rees/Rex Features, bottom left Rex Features, right David Fisher/Rex Features
69 Rex Features
70 talkbackTHAMES
71 Jonathan Hordle/Rex Features

72 Paul Grover/Rex Features
74–75 left to right Nick Randall/Rex Features, ITV/Rex Features, Ken McKay/Rex Features, Jonathan Hordle/Rex Features
76 clockwise from top left ITV/Rex Features, Brad Barket/Getty Images, Ray Tang/Rex Features, Rex Features
78 clockwise from top left Rex Features, Rex Features, Dave Hogan/Getty Images, Scott Barbour/Getty Images
80–81 top Huw John/Rex Features, bottom Mark Campbell/Rex Features
82 left to right Sten Rosenlund/Rex Features, Ken McKay/Rex Features
83 top to bottom ITV/Rex Features, Nils Jorgensen/Rex Features, ITV/Rex Features
84 clockwise from top left Ben Stansall/Getty Images, Ben Stansall/Getty Images, David Fisher/Rex Features, Ben Stansall/Getty Images
85 clockwise from top left David Fisher/Rex Features, Gareth Cattermole/Getty Images, Claire Greenaway/Getty Images
86 Hulton Archive/Getty Images
87 top EMPICS Entertainment/PA Photos bottom David Fisher/Rex Features
89 top to bottom c.Rogue/Everett/Rex Features, c.20th Century Fox/Everett/Rex Features, c.Universal/Everett/Rex Features
90 left to right Frank Micelotta/Getty Images, Gareth Cattermole/Getty Images, Gabriel Bouys/Getty Images
91 c.Miramax/Everettt/Rex Features
92–93 cloclwise from top left c.Warner Bros/Everett/Rex Features, Steve Finn/Getty Images, c.FoxSearch/Everett/Rex Features, c.FoxSearch/Everett/Rex Features, c.Miramax/Everett/Rex Features, c.Dreamworks/Everett/Rex Features

Hitting the Headlines
94–95 AFP/Getty Images, Peter Macdiarmid/Getty Images, PA Wire/PA Photos
96 clockwise from top left Melanie Maps/Getty Images, Jeff J Mitchell/Getty Images, Rex Features, Nick Potts/PA Wire/PA Photos, Rex Features, PA Wire/PA Photos, Denis Doyle/Getty Images
97 clockwise from top left Rex Features, Jonathna Hordle/Rex Features, Albanpix Ltd/Rex Features, Melanie Maps/Getty Images, Matthew Lewis/Getty Images, Rex Features
98 Christopher furlong/Getty Images
99 PA Wire/Pa Photos
100 top Tony Larkie/Rex Features, bottom Geoff Robinson/Rex Features
101 Stuart Clarke/Rex Features
103 Peter Macdiarmid/Getty Images
104 top Peter Macdiarmid/Getty Images, bottom Kieran Dodds/Getty Images
105 Jeff J Mitchell/Getty Images
106 Richard Martin–Roberts/Getty Images
108–109 Daniel Berehulak/Getty Images
110 Paul Grover/Rex Features
111 Nils Jorgensen/Rex Features
112 AP/PA Photos
113 David Silverman/Getty Images
114–115 Heikki Saukkomaa/Rex Features
116–117 Jamie McDonald/Getty Images
118 Shaun Curry/Getty Images
119 PA Wire/PA Photos
120–121 Eurostar
122 LCR/TROIKA
123 Jonathan Hordle/Rex Features
124 top AFP/Getty Images, bottom left Lisa Maree Williams/Getty Images, bottom right PA Archive/PA Photos
125 clockwise from top left Leon Neal/Getty Images, PA Wire/PA Photos, Chris Jackson/Getty Images
127 Getty Images

Politics
130–131 left to right Tom Stoddart/Getty Images, Daniel
Berehulak/Getty Images, AFP/Getty Images
132 clockwise from top left Scott Barbour/Getty Images, Tom
Stoddart Archive/Getty Images, Bruno Vincent/Getty Images,
Scott Barbour/Getty Images, Bruno Vincent/Getty Images, Terry
O'Neil/Getty Images, Peter Macdiarmid/Getty Images, Bruno
Vincent/Getty Images
134 Tom Stoddart Archive/Getty Images
135 top Anwar Hussein Collection/Getty Images, bottom Peter
Macdiarmid/Getty Images
136 Mark Wilson/Getty Images
137 Scott Barbour/Getty Images
138 clockwise from top left Adrian Dennis/Getty Images, Sion
Tonhig/Getty Images, AFP/Getty Images
140 AP/PA Photos
142 Pa Archive/PA Photos
143 Matt Cardy/Getty Images
144 Daniel Berehulak/Getty Images
145 PA Wire/PA Photos
147 Tom Stoddart/Getty Images
148–149 Rex Features

Music and Fashion
150–151 left to right UK Press/PA Photos, Gareth Cattermole/Getty
Images, Pool/Tim Graham/Getty Images
152 top PA Archives/PA Photos, bottom UK Press/PA Photo
153 top Scoopt/Getty Images, bottom left and right EMPICS
Entertainment/PA Photo
154 Dave Hogan/Getty Images
155 EMPICS Entertainment/PA Photos
156 top Pool/Tim Graham/Getty Images, bottom Dave Hogan/Getty
Images
157 AP/PA Photos
158 clockwise from top left James McCauley/Rex Features, Brian
Rasic/Rex Features, Brian Rasic/Rex Features, Matt Cardy/ Brian
Rasic/Rex Features, Gareth Cattermole/Getty Images
159 James McCauley/Rex Features
161 Leon Schadeberg/Rex Features
162 Getty Images
163 clockwise from top left Getty Images, MJ Kim/Getty Images,
Tom Meighan/Getty Images, Carl de Souza/Getty Images
164 Anwar Hussein/Getty Images
165 left to right Frank Micelotta/Getty Images, EMPICS
Entertainment/PA Photos, Rex Features
166 David Silverman/Getty Images
167 Timothy A Clary/Getty Images
168 Adrian Brooks/Rex Features
169 Gareth Cattermole/Getty Images
170 top Peter Macdiarmid/Getty Images, bottom Ray Tang/Rex
Features
172 Dave M Bennett/Getty Images
173 clockwise from top left Gareth Cattermole/Getty Images, PA
Wire/PA Photos, EMPICS Entertainment/PA Photos
174 Dave Hogan/Getty Images
175 clockwise from top left Jim Smeal/BEI/Rex Features, James
McCauley/Rex Features, Chris Jackson/Getty Images, Jim
Smeal/BEI/Rex Features, Matt Baron/Rex Features, Hector
Maton/Getty Images
177 clockwise from top left Jonathan Hordle/Rex Features, Jonathan
Hordle/Rex Features, Ray Tang/Rex Features, PA Archive/PA
Photos, Mark Campbell/Rex Features

Sport
178–179 left to right Ian Watton/Getty Images, Getty Images, Attila
Kisbenedek/Getty Images
180–181 Ryan Pierse/Getty Images
182 BBC
183 John Peters/Getty Images

185 John Peters/Getty Images, Mike Hewitt/Getty Images, Shaun
Botterill/Getty Images
187 top left Jeff J Mitchell/Getty Images, top right EMPICS Sport/PA
Photos, bottom Getty Images
188 top Laurence Griffiths/Getty Images, middle Manchester
City/PA Photos, bottom Phil Cole/Getty Images
189 left to right Jeff J Michell/Getty Images, Gary M Prior/Getty
Images
190 Richard Heathcote/Getty Images
191 clockwise from top left Phil Cole/Getty Images, John
Peters/Getty Images, Ian Watton/Getty Images, Phil Cole/Getty
Images, Nicholas Asfouri/Getty Images, Chris Young/Getty
Images
192 clockwise from top left Richard Saker/Rex Features, Mark
Thompson/Getty Images, MJ Kim/Getty Images, Bryn
Lennon/Getty Images
193 Clive Mason/Getty Images
194 top left Martin Bureau/Getty Images, top right William
West/Getty Images, bottom Fred Dufour/Getty Images
197 Shaun Botterill/Getty Images
198 top John Gichigi/Getty Images, bottom Stu Forster/Getty
Images
199 top Christopher Lee/Getty Images, bottom Stu Forster/Getty
Images
200 top and bottom left Ray Tang/Rex Features, right Richard
Heathcote/Getty Images
201 left Michael Dunlea/Getty Images, right AP/PA Photos
202 Clive Rose/Getty Images
203 Hamish Blur/Getty Images
204 Saeed Khan/Getty Images
206 Michael Steel/Getty Images
207 top Bryn Lennon/Getty Images, bottom Etham Miller/Getty
Images
208–209 left to right Stringer/Getty Images, Julian Finney/Getty
Images, Julian Herbert/Getty Images, Clive Rose/Getty Images
210 clockwise from top left Pool/Getty Images, Stringer/Getty
Images, Clive Brunskill/Getty Images
211 Julian Finney/Getty Images
212 Darren Carroll/Getty Images
213 Stuart Franklin/Getty Images

Farewell
214–215 from left to right PA Wire/PA Photos, Rex Features, Rex
Features
216 Rex Features
217 Rex Features
218 Rex Features
219 Ged Murray/Rex Features
220 top Fox Photos/Getty Images, bottom AP/PA Photos
221 from top to bottom Laski Diffusion–Wojtek/Getty Images,
Kristain Dowling/Getty Images, ITV/Rex Features, Richard
Saker/Rex Features

Cover:
Lewis Hamilton: Rex Features;
Harry Potter book: Lisa Maree Williams/Getty Images;
Madeleine McCann: Rex Features;
Northern Rock: courtesy of Northern Rock;
Tony Blair: Peter Macdiarmid/Getty Images
Flood: Christopher Furlong/Getty Images
Amy Winehouse: EMPICS Entertainment/PA Photos;
Jonny Wilkinson: Getty Images

Additional research and writing by Tom Bryant and Carrie Dunn